The Perfect Shot:
Mini Edition for Africa II

BY
KEVIN "DOCTARI" ROBERTSON

To our daughters, Samantha, Natalie, and Purdey
and grandchildren, Alexia Lila, Jade Amelia, and Hunter.

May the wild places of Africa and the game animals therein be enjoyed by your children's children.

The trademark Safari Press ® is registered with the U.S. Patent and Trademark Office and in other countries.

Robertson, Kevin

First edition

Safari Press Inc.

2016, Long Beach, California

ISBN 978-1-57157-462-6

Library of Congress Catalog Card Number: 2002107791

10 9 8 7 6 5 4 3

Printed in China

Readers wishing to see Safari Press's many fine books on big-game hunting, wingshooting, and sporting firearms should visit our website at www.safaripress.com.

CONTENTS

ACKNOWLEDGMENTS

To Catherine, my wife, for her wonderful photographs and ideas, love and continuous support through thick and thin. And to Cathy Nel, for once again producing a wonderful set of anatomy diagrams. Without you both, this work would never have seen the light of day.

To Charlie Brittz for his frontal lion and black rhino photos and to Richard Sowry for his leopard photos.

ABBREVIATIONS AND REFERENCES

Throughout the text and appendixes of this book, *Safari Club International's Record Book of Trophy Animals* is abbreviated as SCI and *Rowland Ward's Records of Big Game* is abbreviated as RW. An explanation of SCI and RW measurement methods (referred to throughout text as numbers in parentheses) is given in Appendixes II and III.

INTRODUCTION

"Within reason, where you hit a game animal is more important than what you hit it with" is an often quoted and very true statement. The reason for it is simple—correct first-shot placement, with a suitable size and adequately constructed bullet, is, without a doubt, the most important criterion for successful, and therefore enjoyable, sport hunting, regardless of the species concerned.

To accomplish this, a thorough knowledge of any game animal's sex, habits, and habitat is essential. Even more so is knowing the internal bodily positions of all the "vital for immediate life" organs—the heart, lungs, brain, and spinal column—from all angles.

It is, therefore, my hope that this booklet will serve to illustrate this knowledge to the sport hunter of African game animals and, in so doing, help him or her to do so well, enjoyably, and ethically.

No shot at heart/lung area when front leg is in rearward position because the solid humerus bone covers much of the heart.

THE AFRICAN ELEPHANT
Loxodonta africana

Natural History — Member of the Big Five and the world's largest land mammal. Weighs up to seven tons and stands eleven feet or more at the shoulder. Dark gray skin provides excellent camouflage. Extremely nimble and fast for its size. Eyesight relatively poor, sense of smell phenomenal, hearing also very good. Walks great distances daily. Voracious and destructive feeders. Life expectancy 50 to 70 years. Preferred diet is grass. Has a daily food requirement of 500 pounds. Drinks regularly.

Sex Determination — Cows have a smaller body and thin, slender tusks; cows exhibit an almost 90-degree angle to foreheads. Mature bulls have large heads in relation to body size, with forehead rounded, not angled. Bulls usually found on their own or in company of a few other bulls and only occasionally with a herd of cows. Tuskless cows and those with young calves at side can be extremely aggressive.

Trophy Assessment — Ivory grows throughout life, so the older the elephant, the better the ivory. Old ivory also is denser, with a smaller nerve cavity. To judge weight of ivory, estimate diameter of tusk at lip in inches and multiply times three; that equals the circumference of tusk at lip. Multiply this, in feet, by estimated length of tusk along outside of curve from lip to tip and subtract 5 percent. Answer will be tusk's approximate weight in pounds. (Straight line from eye to lip is 2 feet.) SCI method (14); RW method (16).

The Hunt — Involves finding the right spoor and then tracking. You hunt an elephant with your legs! Toenail scuffmarks point forward, indicating direction of travel. Spoor size indicates body size and also age. Droppings are used to determine how close you are getting. Fresh dung is strong smelling, warm, wet, and yellowish green in color; changes to walnut brown as outer surface dries. Wind direction very important. Move slowly and quietly. Get in close for the first shot. Fifty paces is considered a long shot and 20–30 paces is about average.

Rifle, Caliber, and Bullet Selection — The legal minimum is the .375. Use only good-quality 300- or 350-grain solids. Little margin for shot-placement error with any caliber. For more knockdown effect, the various .40 calibers and 400- to 450-grain solids are a better option. The .458s and 500- or 550-grain solids at 2,150 fps are the best choice for clients while for PHs, if recoil is manageable, the various .500s with 525- to 600-grain solids provide the best "backup."

Shot Placement — Side-on high heart/lung shot is safest with greatest margin for error. Top of heart and center of lungs are a hand's width above and in front of the front leg "crease." Take no shot when the front leg is positioned rearward as it covers heart with solid bone. Brain shot is impressive but difficult for the inexperienced. Side-on brain shot easier: Place in lower half of ear hole. Remember to compensate for upward-shooting angle if head is held higher than shooter's eye level. Frontal brain shot more difficult and depends entirely on position of head at time of shot. Imagine a broomstick through ear holes. Shoot to cut broomstick in half. Hind legs always collapse first when brain shot successful. When front legs give way first, elephant only knocked out. Insurance shots are important. Always shoot again any elephant that drops to the shot. From the rear, a spinal shot is a good option as a backing shot and so is breaking a hip joint. A raking body shot is best when the elephant is angled away.

Anatomy diagram

The ear-hole opening into the skull is level with the top of the eye. This corresponds with the bottom of the outer ear-hole slit, at the back edge of the zygomatic arches.

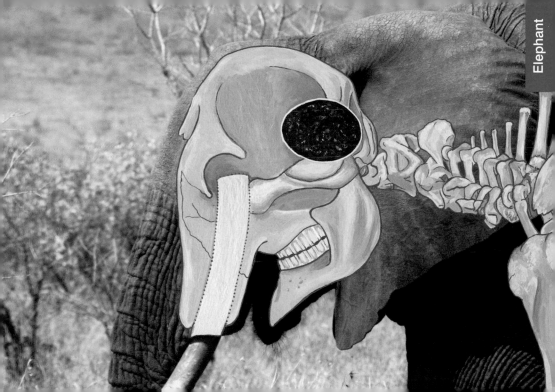

The rumen and spleen lie on the left-hand side. The top-of-the-heart shot gives more "one-shot-kills" than any other.

Buffalo

BUFFALO
Syncerus caffer

Natural History — One of the Big Five. This dangerous game animal can be aggressive, vindictive, and cunning, especially when wounded. Can weigh up to three-quarters of a ton. Has exceptional eyesight, hearing, and sense of smell. Gregarious herd animals. Water-dependent coarse grazers and occasional browsers. Favors thick bush during daylight; grazes early mornings and late afternoons. Old bulls are best trophies.

Sex Determination — Can be difficult when visibility is restricted. Both sexes carry horns, but cows do not have a boss. Mature bulls have thick, well-muscled necks, heavy, well-developed shoulders, blunt horn tips, a solid boss, and a distinctly visible penis sheath. A bull's spoor much bigger than that of a cow's. Lone animals invariably are old bulls.

Trophy Assessment — Look for wide outside spread, deep curl, and a solid boss. Ear-tip to ear-tip spread is 32–33 inches. A hand's width (4 inches) of spread on both sides will be a trophy in the 40-inch bracket—an exceptional trophy. Younger breeding bulls usually score better than old bulls. For the preservation of trophy quality, breeding or herd bulls should not be sport hunted. SCI method (4); RW method (12).

The Hunt — Track, walk, and stalk. Buffalo need to drink daily; this makes finding spoor easier. Warmth and freshness of dung is a good indicator of how far ahead they are. Watch/listen for oxpeckers, the hunter's friend. Need to check the wind constantly as sense of smell excellent. First and last light are buffalo "stupid hours" when it is easier to approach them. Get in close—30 to 80 paces is usual shooting distance. Easily killed with good expanding-type bullet through top of heart/center of lungs.

Rifle, Caliber, and Bullet Selection—Legal minimum is 9.3x62mm, 9.3x74R, or .375s H&H, with 286- to 350-grain bullets. Heavy for caliber, premium-quality expanding bullets work best for the first shot. Follow-up or backing shots to be taken with solids or cup-nose solids. Larger calibers, .40s, and .458s with 400- to 550-grain bullets more effective. Good-quality, low-power variable scope an advantage in thick bush. First shot is *extremely important* so rifle/caliber/cartridge combination must be "shootable." The word *shootable* means not too much recoil.

Shot Placement — Side-on high heart/lung shot the surest/most recommended: Place shot into center of the "vital triangle." Full frontal or quartering shots more common and very effective if placed correctly. Place full-frontal, heart/lung shot squarely into center of chest. Use shoulder joints as reference point. Top of heart and all the "plumbing" at this level. Place shot a bit higher for full-frontal spinal shot. Quartering frontal shot depends on angle: Place either on shoulder joint or just inside it. Quartering-away shots: Should be taken only as backup shots and only from buffalo's right-hand side—NEVER from left-hand side as this is where rumen is situated. Use solids and get angle right. Side-on, neck/spinal shot just in front and above shoulder joint in middle of neck. Little margin for shot-placement error but will result in a drop-to-the-shot effect. Side-on, shoulder/spinal shot placed through shoulder blade. Full frontal brain shot depends on angle of head: When nose lifted, place on bridge of nose. Full-frontal neck shot when head down: place shot on neck's midline. Rear-end or "Texas heart shot" placed just above anus at base of tail

Anatomy diagram.

Buffalo

Buffalo

The frontal, head down position offers the center-of-the-chest, top-of-the-heart shot, and the frontal brain shot.

Frontal anatomy diagram. Notice the centrally situated heart and how low the spinal column dips beneath the chin.

Hippopotamus

The thick, blubbery skin and barrel roundness of a hippo's body makes identifying the shoulder bones and vital triangle difficult. Rather, use the back edge of the front leg for the orientation of a high heart/lung shot. The ear base is the location for the side brain shot.

HIPPOPOTAMUS
Hippopotamus amphibius

Natural History — This herbivore has four distinct toes on each foot. Lives 30 to 40 years. Nocturnal grazing animal; leaves the safety of water at night to graze. Front teeth used for threatening displays and fighting. Bristle-covered lips used for grazing. Can weigh up to three tons and consumes in excess of one hundred pounds of herbage per night. Social animal found in pods that average ten to fifteen members. Not a good swimmer; runs along bottom instead. Fast on land—can run eighteen miles per hour. When alarmed, heads for safety of deep water by shortest possible route and is dangerous when this happens. Cows with young calves especially dangerous, so approach with extreme caution.

Sex Determination — Mature bulls have broader, longer, and generally bigger heads in relation to overall body size; necks also thicker and more muscular. More violin shape to head as a result of lower-tusk, upper-lip "bumps." When they are submerged, the only way to determine sex is to evaluate head size and observe the pod carefully. Dominant bull will usually be on fringes of pod, performing open-mouth threatening displays.

Trophy Assessment — A hippo's tusks (two lower incisor teeth) are its impressive trophies. Field judging trophy quality is difficult as half the tusk's length is embedded in lower jawbone. Lower incisors wear against the uppers and is what keeps them sharp and short. Exceptional trophies occur when the upper incisor is deformed or damaged. SCI method (12); RW method (5).

The Perfect Shot: Mini Edition for Africa II

The Hunt — Usually illegal to hunt at night or with a spotlight. Since hippos are usually found in or next to water during legal shooting hours, the hunter's own conscience must decide ethics for a fair-chase hunt. Not easy to approach on land because of good eyesight, keen sense of hearing, relatively good sense of smell. Ambushing a basking hippo on a bank or stalking an identified bull as it basks in the sun are the most ethical hunting methods. Many wounded hippos are lost if they get back to flowing water. Bodies are particularly dense; therefore, when killed, the hippo sinks immediately—but will float an hour or two later when the stomach bloats.

Rifle, Caliber, and Bullet Selection — Hippos have huge bodies and thick skins. Legal minimum is the .375s or the various 9.3mms. The .40s and .458s with 400- and 500-grain solids are essentially for body shots because hunters are often not accurate enough to make brain shots with these calibers. For brain shots, good-quality softpoints work best. A suitable scope is essential for the precise shot placement that is required for brain shots.

Shot Placement — Side-on high heart/lung shot is most effective if hippo is far from running water: Come up back edge of front leg and place shot between one-third and halfway up the body on that line. Thick blubbery skin makes identifying "vital triangle" or shoulder blade difficult; it also makes spinal shots hard to place accurately/correctly. The brain shot is the only option when hippo is in water: Place at base of ear or an inch or two in front of ear base. Frontal brain shot: Place above inverted "V" (Λ) at level of ear bases.

The Perfect Shot: Mini Edition for Africa II

Anatomy diagram.

Hippopotamus

Hippopotamus

In the frontal head-down position, the inverted V (Λ) formed by the hippo's bulging eye sockets is easy to see. The front edge of the brain corresponds to vertex point of the Λ.

The base of the ears is the marker for the brain shot.

Hippopotamus

The side-on high heart/lung shot is the most effective.

Rhinoceros

RHINOCEROS
Ceratotherium simum (White), Diceros bicornis (Black)

Natural History — One of the Big Five. White rhinos have square lips, and black rhinos have a hook lip. White rhinos are considerably larger than black rhinos and have longer, broader, more prehistoric-looking head; square muzzle; and prominent hump in the neck and shoulder region. Exclusively grazing animals that eat grass only; lifespan up to 40 years. Social and relatively docile; aggressive only when actively courting or protecting young. Can weigh as much as 2½ tons.

Black rhinos are smaller in overall body size (a mature bull will weigh about a ton) with shorter head, rounder ears, and distinct prehensile or hooked upper lip. Almost exclusively woody browsers. More temperamental than the white; may charge without provocation. Both types carry two continuously growing "horns," which are really dense, hairlike skin outgrowths.

Sex Determination — Difficult to determine with white rhinos as some mature females attain the huge size of old males. A female's horns may be longer than a male's, but the bases will be smaller. Behavior upon defecation and urination is also a key because males urinate backward. Checking the area below the tail is the best way to be certain of a rhino's sex.

Trophy Assessment — Horn length of 25 inches = good; 28 inches = excellent; 30 = exceptional. Average bases: 22 to 24 inches. Look for big bases and easily visible good length. SCI method (8): length of both horns + circumference of both horns at bases. RW method (15): length of longest horn.

The Perfect Shot: Mini Edition for Africa II

Rhinoceros

The Hunt — White rhinos most expensive of Big Five to hunt. Classified as dangerous but usually relatively docile. Dominant breeding bulls are strongly territorial, always walk the same well-worn paths. Spoor large and easy to find. Grazing animals. Rhinos spend the first and last few hours of daylight feeding in the open and are easy to spot from a distance. Have phenomenal hearing, good sense of smell, but poor eyesight. Relatively easy to approach if wind is right and the stalk is quiet.

Rifle, Caliber, and Bullet Selection — Rhinos are considered pachyderms with good reason—their skin is incredibly thick. Regardless of caliber, only the very best-quality solid bullets should be used. The .375s and 300-grain solids are the legal minimum. The .40s with 400-grain solids or .458s with 500-grain solids are a better, more effective option.

Shot Placement — A high heart/lung shot from full broadside position is shot of choice: Come up a hand's length above the prominent skin fold on the front leg; the line of the rear edge of the front leg will be the top of the heart and the center of the lungs. Quartering frontal shot: Place shot inside front shoulder at that level. On charging rhino use only brain shot. Backing shots (from the rear) are placed above root of tail.

Anatomy diagram of a white rhino.

Rhinoceros

Quartering frontal shot.

Frontal brain shot.

Rhinoceros

Lion

When the front leg is in the forward position, the heart is well exposed.

LION
Panthera leo

Natural History — One of the Big Five and Africa's largest feline; weighs between 400 and 500 pounds, stands nearly 4 feet at shoulder; and has an overall length up to 10 feet. Lions have retractable, talonlike claws. Lionesses are somewhat smaller, weighing 250 to 300 pounds; they are generally more aggressive than males. Mature lions have little fear of man and are especially bold during darkness. Superb night vision. Lionesses with cubs particularly aggressive. Lion prey on virtually all of the continent's antelope species.

Sex Determination — Only males have manes; mane starts to develop between 2½ and 3 years. Some males remain maneless but are generally larger than females and have thicker, heavier-set necks and more heavily muscled shoulders. Only males older than six years should be hunted and then only if not a pride male.

Trophy Assessment — Mane on exceptional lion will cover the shoulders and frontal chest area completely and may even extend down to the elbows and along belly line. Skull measured for record book; SCI method (15) and RW method (17).

The Hunt — Baiting is the most commonly practiced method to hunt lions. They have huge appetites and can consume up to 25 percent of own body weight in single feeding, and, thus, large quantities of meat are needed for baiting purposes. Zebra favorite bait, followed by buffalo and hippo, but will feed on virtually any kind of meat. Hang bait at least six feet above ground from a tree in the center of an open area with good, all-round visibility. Lions will usually feed on bait when it's dark. Catch them on bait at first light (half-hour before sunrise) or when they arrive at last light. Tracking lions not all that difficult as they like to walk on roads, sandy riverbeds, and game trails. Tracking to daytime resting place also a good hunting method.

Rifle, Caliber, and Bullet Selection — A 7mm that produces 3,000 ft-lbs of muzzle energy is the legal minimum in some African countries; in others, it's the .375s. With smaller calibers, use heaviest, good-quality softpoint bullet available. With larger calibers, choose softpoint bullets that will expand relatively quickly. Good scope essential for all low-light conditions. For wounded lion follow-up , bigger is definitely better: Use .40 or .458 calibers with heavy, quick-expanding bullets. An open, express-sighted double is the best rifle choice for follow-up.

Shot Placement — Side-on high heart/lung shot surest and most recommended: Place shot well back behind shoulder, on or just below the body's horizontal midline. High shoulder/spinal shot will drop a lion; the spine lies directly beneath middle of shoulder blade. Brain shot not recommended as skull measured for record books. Full frontal shot: Place shot squarely into center of chest. A rear-end shot is for backup only: Place at base of tail just above anus. Shooting is NOT recommended when lion is lying down—known as the "sphinx position." Shoulders move even farther forward in this position, which distorts position of internal organs.

Anatomy diagram.

Lion

Lion

Full-frontal chest shot.

Frontal brain shot.

Lion

Leopard

High heart/lung and shoulder/spinal shots are the two most effective options from side-on. The latter will drop a leopard; the former may not.

LEOPARD
Panthera pardus

Natural History — Smallest in body size and most widely distributed of Africa's Big Five; extremely dangerous when wounded. Solitary animals, live in isolation, and are primarily nocturnal. Can live without water if necessary by getting their moisture requirements from prey but will drink regularly if water available. Mature tom weighs between 120 and 180 pounds, female 70 to 130 pounds. Strongly territorial. Prey on virtually any meat source; will also scavenge; likes rotten meat. Life expectancy 12 to 15 years.

Sex Determination — Difficult to determine sex. Mature toms are large, thickset, and well muscled. Heads larger in relation to overall size. Mature females slender, not as well muscled; heads smaller, slimmer necks. Male and female rarely seen together, so difficult to compare. Look for testicles below tail, which are easily visible on a trophy-size tom.

Trophy Assessment — Body length (nose to tip of tail) used to determine size: >7 feet = good trophy and >8 feet = huge. Size of spoor an aid to determining body size: Trophy leopard's spoor is 3½ to 4 inches in length. SCI method (15); RW method (17).

The Hunt — Search for a suitable-size spoor in areas where favored prey most abundant: near waterholes, pans, and river pools. Select blind site carefully—to be able to get in and out unseen—and hang bait. Bait tree must not be too exposed at base. Easy access to blind most important. Impala usually make best bait as do warthog and bushpig. Drag bait area well, but do not overdo "scent." Build blind 50–120 paces downwind once bait has been fed on. Stable shooting rest in blind most important. Sit dead still since leopard have phenomenal eyesight and hearing. Communicate only by gestures. In dry, sandy areas, tracking also used as a hunting method.

Rifle, Caliber, and Bullet Selection — A 7mm is as low as one should go. In some African countries various 9.3mms or .375s are minimum legal calibers for all dangerous game, including leopard. Bullets suitable for leopard must be quick expanding so as to release kinetic energy (hydrostatic shock) rapidly and create a large, permanent wound channel. A good-quality, light-gathering scope with an illuminated reticle is essential.

Shot Placement — Leopards are particularly susceptible to hydrostatic shock. Heart is positioned well back in chest cavity. Side-on high heart/lung shot very effective, but not immediately so: Place shot well behind shoulder and halfway up body where elbow reaches when front leg is at its most rearward position when walking. High shoulder/spinal shots are used to "drop" a leopard and are a good choice for "last-light" situations. Place shot through center of shoulder blade; this is also a good option when leopard is in "dog-sitting" position. Quartering toward shot: Place right on shoulder joint. Full-frontal shot: Place squarely into center of chest. Quartering-away shots: Aim to break opposite shoulder. Shots taken at leopard lying on a branch or ground are not recommended.

The Perfect Shot: Mini Edition for Africa II

Leopard

Side-on anatomy diagram.

In the dog-sitting position, the same options apply.

Leopard

Dog sitting anatomy diagram.

Leopard

The brain lies between the eye and ear ridge, above the bend on the "smile." The spine lies in the middle of the neck, beyond the tip of the smile.

Crocodile

NILE CROCODILE
Crocodylus niloticus

Natural History — Shy, wary, and cautious, these cold-blooded reptiles lay eggs, are nocturnal feeders, spend hours of darkness in water, and feed primarily on fish. Long-living, slow-growing creatures. Trophy-size specimens will be 75 to 100 years old. Bull crocodiles are strongly territorial when fully mature/dominant. Difficult to approach on foot within a reasonable shooting distance.

Sex Determination — Big bull crocodiles will have a large, noticeably broad head and wide, well-rounded, V-shape muzzle. Entire head will have a dark knobby appearance, receded gums, and distinctly visible teeth. Necks will be thick, broad, and muscular, with well-developed, fleshy jowls to the sides. Eyes relatively far apart. Female's head more slender, muzzle parallel sided. Females rarely longer than 12 feet.

Trophy Assessment — Estimate straight-line length in inches, from nostrils to eyes; this length in inches approximately equals body length in feet. Regardless of sex, 12 feet = good trophy, >13 feet = very good, >14 feet = exceptional, and >15 feet = phenomenal. SCI method (16C); RW method (18):

The Hunt — Challenging to hunt. They see, hear, and smell extremely well; they are also able to detect ground vibrations and have "feathered watchdogs." Absolutely precise first-shot placement essential to "anchor" a big croc successfully. Ambush known basking site. Baiting the most successful hunting method. Secure bait at water's edge. Use any form of meat as bait. Replenish daily until territorial bull has eaten his fill and lies next to bait to guard it. Build blind downwind. Shooting distance: longest range at which a golf-ball-size target can be hit with the chosen rifle/caliber/scope combination (50–80 paces). Stable shooting rest essential (sandbags). Measure blind to bait distance carefully, and sight rifle in for this distance.

Rifle, Caliber, and Bullet Selection — A trophy-size croc requires a surgically precise first-shot placement, so selection must be capable of this. The 7mms or .30 caliber with premium-quality softpoint bullets a sensible minimum. Larger calibers of 9.3mms and .375s with good 300-grain softpoints a better choice if sufficiently accurate. Quality expanding softpoints essential; use solids for follow-up shots into the shoulders and hips. Good scope also essential: 1.5–5X or 1.75–6X a good choice.

Shot Placement — "Anchoring" first shot requires knowledge of skull and neck. Brain is golf-ball size and lies midway between eyes and ear ridges, two inches below eye level. Side-on brain shot: Depending on angle, place shot just above the "L" bend of the smile. Side-on neck/spinal shot: Place shot at end of "smile" and in middle of neck; compensate for downward-shooting angle when the croc is below eye level. Full frontal shot: Place bullet on midline, slightly behind eyes. Full going-away shot: Place shot behind head, on midline. Backup shots: Place through shoulders and hips. Use solids for backup shots.

Side-on, head-only anatomy diagram.

Crocodile

On a fully broadside hyena, come up the center of the foreleg and place a high heart/lung shot on that line at the height of the shoulder joint. Place a shoulder/spinal shot higher and farther forward on the shoulder as indicated to the right.

Hyena

SPOTTED HYENA
Crocuta crocuta

Natural History — These strange-looking, doglike creatures were considered vermin for many years. Spotted hyena most common species; striped hyena *(Hyaena hyaena)* and brown hyena *(Hyaena brunnea)* also found locally. Scavengers but also effective and cunning predators. Their giggles and whoops are the sounds of Africa. They will eat almost anything, raid camps, and can be a real nuisance. Mainly active at night, but will scavenge and feed during daylight when the opportunity arises. Weigh 100 to 190 pounds. Tall, powerful shoulders, muscular neck, weak and sloping hindquarters. They are poor jumpers. Social animals, living in family groups or clans. Females dominant.

Sex Determination — Very difficult to determine sex. No sex specified on the hunting permit or license because of this. Originally thought to be hermaphrodites. Only way to determine sex is to compare body size if more than one animal present. Females bigger and heavier than males.

Trophy Assessment — Goes on body size = good head and skull size. SCI method (15) is combined length and greatest width of skull in inches; RW method (17) is length of skull added to width of skull.

The Hunt — Can be a real challenge. Hyenas are primarily nocturnal and are shy and elusive. Can be very cautious and wary when hunted regularly. Hunting at night or by torchlight illegal in most African countries.

Hyena

Only way to hunt hyenas successfully during legal shooting hours is to bait them. Build a blind and be in it at least an hour before sunset or first shooting light. Use any large animal carcass for bait and secure it just out of reach so that hyenas will "hang around."

Rifle, Caliber, and Bullet Selection — Any rifle/caliber/scope combination suitable for the majority of Africa's medium-size antelopes will do: the various 7mms or .30 calibers with conventional softpoint bullets. A good scope with a well-defined or illuminated reticle is essential for the low-light conditions in which most shots at hyenas will be taken.

Shot Placement — Side-on high heart/lung shot most effective: Sight up the front leg and place shot squarely on body's horizontal midline. If not immediately effective, hyena may escape to underground den. High shoulder/spinal shot: Shoot farther forward and higher up the shoulder, through center of shoulder blade, and hyena should drop to the shot. Frontal shots: Place bullet squarely into center of chest at base of neck between shoulder joints. Quartering shots: Be sure to get angles right so bullet either stays in or passes through chest cavity. Head shots: Avoid if skull is to be measured for record-book purposes.

Anatomy diagram.

Hyena

Giraffe

High heart/lung, high neck/spinal and brain shots are indicated.

GIRAFFE
Giraffa camelopardalis

Natural History — Translation of *camelopardalis* is "the body size and shape of a camel and the spots of a leopard." Tallest and heaviest of the world's hoofed animals. Mature bulls stand as tall as 19 feet; an average giraffe can weigh 1½ tons. Giraffes have two short, skin-covered, callous-tipped, bony "horns" on top of head; these "horns" larger and better developed in mature males. Subspecies differ in hide color and pattern. They are predominantly browsers that feed mainly during daylight hours. They never lie flat on the ground and rarely sleep. Have very keen eyesight. Docile by nature but will defend themselves when attacked, using front feet. Man and lion their only predators. Loosely associated herd structure.

Sex Determination — Mature giraffe bulls are considerably larger and almost twice as heavy as even the biggest of cows; they are also considerably darker in color. Mature bulls emit an offensive, musty odor (known as "stink bulls"); have bigger, better-developed "horns"; and a median horn in the middle of the forehead. Penis sheath clearly visible on the bottom of the belly line. Mature cows rarely encountered alone while bulls are usually solitary.

Trophy Assessment — Not recorded in any of the record books.

The Hunt — Giraffes have exceptionally keen eyesight, acute hearing, and cautious dispositions. The terrain in which they are found can make approaching them a real challenge. They are great wanderers and can cover large distances each day. Neither water dependent nor territorial. Cloven hoofs and considerable body weight create distinctive spoor. Hunt by either spot and stalk or track, walk, and stalk.

Rifle, Caliber, and Bullet Selection — Giraffes have thick, tough skin and they require the same bullet selection as for a pachyderm. Although the hotter 7mms are legal, the 9.3mms or .375s and quality solids are the minimum calibers recommended for all body shots. Larger calibers even more effective. Premium-quality expanding bullets more effective for spinal and brain shots. Solids for body shots regardless of caliber.

Shot Placement — The brain, which is surprisingly small, is positioned beneath and between the two "horns," between the ears and eyes. The heart lies in the center of the chest cavity, far forward and high up. The two prominent bulges on front edge of chest cavity are the shoulder joints. Top of heart lies above these bulges on the vertical line of the front leg. Lungs also positioned well forward and high up in chest cavity. To make a heart/lung shot: Place shot on center line of foreleg, above shoulder "bumps." Heart/lung shot most effective and recommended. Brain shot: Place shot between ear and eye, below "horns." Remember to compensate for upward shooting angle. Low neck/spinal shot: Place shot in center of neck, where it joins body. High neck/spinal shot: Place through center of neck where it joins head. Frontal chest shot: Shoot between and slightly above prominent shoulder joints. Quartering-frontal shots: Aim to break the prominent shoulder joint. Quartering-away shots: Take only as a last resort as heart and lungs are situated high up in chest cavity.

For eland, the high heart/lung shot is the most effective and recommended.

Eland

ELAND
Taurotragus oryx (common), Taurotragus derbianus (giant)

Natural History — There are two species of eland—the common and the giant. They are the largest of Africa's horned antelopes and can outweigh a mature buffalo. Not territorial; great wanderers. Extremely wary, alert, and cautious. Impressive jumpers; manmade barriers are no obstacle. Mixed feeders, browse more than graze, and require a high-protein diet. Drink when water is freely available but can survive on the moisture they obtain from their diet. Gregarious herd animals. Herds occasionally number in the hundreds. Up to three subspecies of common eland and two subspecies of giant eland recognized.

Sex Determination — Both sexes carry spiral, ridged horns, but those of mature bulls are thicker and more massive. A bull's horns are thick and V-shaped; cow horns are thinner, more parallel, vertical, and often deformed. Trophy eland called "blue bulls"; name derived from blue color that develops with advanced age in neck, head, and shoulder areas. Bulls larger, better muscled, and generally more massive than cows, with well-developed, square-edged dewlap at bottom edge of neck. Forehead usually covered with thick mat of hair.

Trophy Assessment — Horns of the giant species considerably thicker, longer, and more impressive looking. Look for good length and mass. Prominent spiral ridge adds inches to the score. The longer and more massive, the better. Good bases are 10 to 13 inches. SCI method (2): length of both horns around spiral ridge + circumference of both horns at bases. RW method (8): length of longest horn.

The Hunt — Chance encounter while out hunting some other game species is only easy way to hunt. Pursuit of trophy bulls difficult. Find suitable spoor and track, walk, and stalk. This alert and wary species is difficult to approach within shooting distance. Bulls most often shot in relatively thick cover at close range.

Rifle, Caliber, and Bullet Selection — A good choice for thick-bush situations: quick-pointing double rifle in either O/U or S/S configuration, in 9.3x74R caliber or .375 flanged with good quality 286- to 300-grain softpoint bullets. Alternative 9.3mm or .375 turnbolt and good-quality, heavy-for-caliber expanding bullets. Use solids for backup shots. Hot 7mms legal minimum but are considered by many PHs to be "too small" for trophy eland. The .40s and 400-grain expanding bullets are a very effective option. Many consider the .375s and good 300-grain expanding bullets the ideal "eland" combination. Essential to have a good scope.

Shot Placement — Side-on, top-of-the-heart/lung shot is the most effective and the one recommended. Place on center line of foreleg, no higher than midway up body. Shoulder/spinal shot is also effective. Place shot higher up on shoulder, through scapula. Quartering-frontal shots: Place bullet to hit shoulder joint. Use solids with backing shots and get the angles correct.

Side-on anatomy diagram.

Eland

The center of the "vital triangle," high heart/lung shot, and shoulder/spinal shots are shown.

Greater Kudu

GREATER KUDU
Tragelaphus strepsiceros

Natural History — Majestic, strikingly beautiful, striped, spiral-horned antelope. This relatively large and heavy but perfectly camouflaged antelope is nicknamed "gray ghost of Africa." It is sly, secretive, and elusive and has exceptional senses. Cows give a warning bark when danger is sensed. Almost exclusively browsers but will graze occasionally. Preferred habitat is rocky, hilly, or mountainous areas interspersed with woodland or thick bush. Kudus drink regularly and are never far from water, but can be encountered in some extremely arid areas. Highly adaptable and excellent jumpers. Gregarious herd animals. Great wanderers. Loves many agricultural crops. Five subspecies recognized.

Sex Determination — Easy to determine sex as only kudu bulls carry horns. Females are tan/brown; bulls are usually dark gray.

Trophy Assessment — Field estimation difficult. Depth of curl varies, and this affects measurement scores significantly: larger curl, more inches, better score. Base circumferences of a good set of horns should measure between 10½ and 12 inches each. Length of the spiral horn in low 50s is fairly common; 55+ really good trophy; 60+ exceptional. Deep curls do not look as impressive as longer horns with shallower curls, but these score better. SCI method (2): length of both horns around spiral ridge + circumference of both horns at bases. RW method (8): length of longest horn.

The Hunt — There are several hunting methods used for kudu: Glass likely feeding spots early in the morning, assess the terrain, and stalk. Ambush a known feeding field in an agricultural area at first light or as kudus return to high ground. Kudus are regular drinkers that like to drink during the heat of day; ambush them on the move to or from a waterhole. Can be tracked in sandy areas. Still-hunting through thick cover is also successful.

Rifle, Caliber, and Bullet Selection — The .270s, 7x57mm, .308 Winchester, and .30-06 with quality controlled-expansion softpoint bullets in 150-, 175-, 180-, and 220-grain weights, respectively, are as small a caliber and light a bullet that can be recommended. Good scope essential for longer shots.

Shot Placement — Neck or head shot can ruin a shoulder mount. High heart/lung shot most recommended: Place shot through center of vital triangle (triangle formed by shoulder blade, point of shoulder, and elbow joint). High, behind the shoulder lung shot recommended for the biltong hunter: Place shot just behind shoulder, above horizontal midline. Quartering-toward shots: Place on or just inside shoulder joint. Going-away shots more difficult as kudu have narrow bodies and slab sides, so consider this shot placement only as last resort.

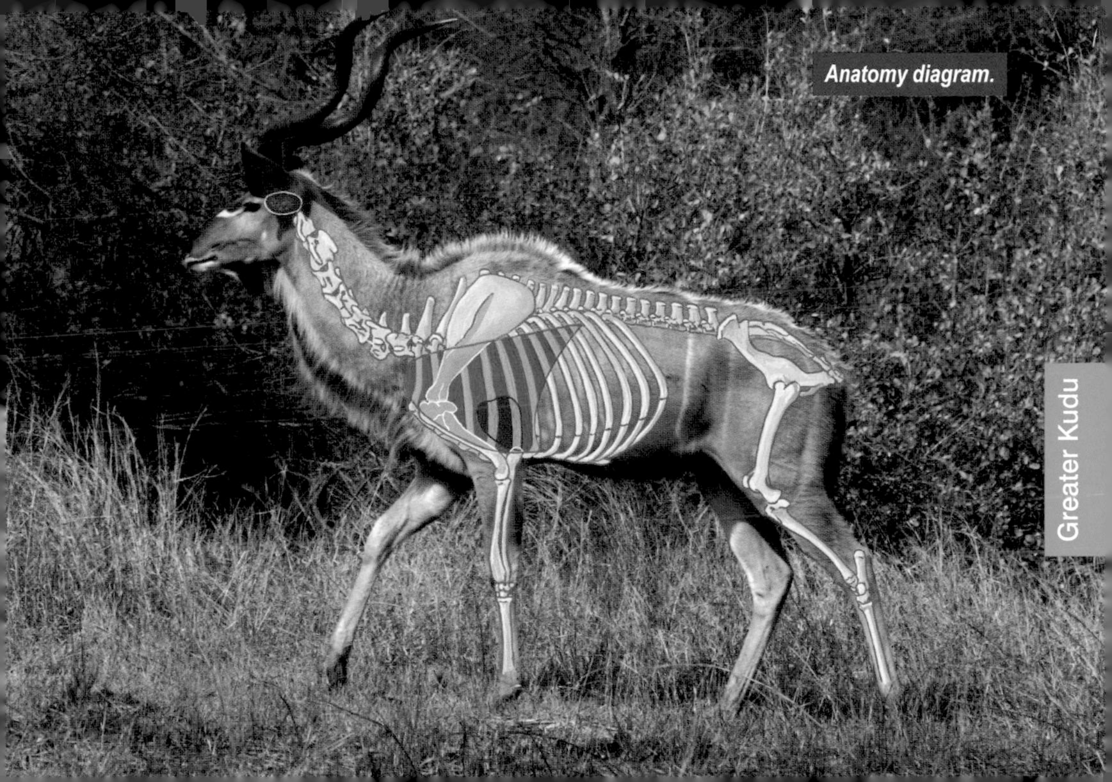
Anatomy diagram.
Greater Kudu

In the shoulder area, a zebra's stripe is often split to form an inverted "Y" (λ). This is a good indicator for the position for a high heart/lung shot.

Zebra

ZEBRA
Equus spp.

Natural History — Sport hunted for their skin and as source of bait for both lion and leopard. Can weigh over 700 pounds. Extremely efficient grazers, so zebras are always fat. Even though they can occur in extremely arid areas, they are water dependent and never far from water. These gregarious herd animals are most often encountered in small family units. They are slow-maturing and long-living animals. Stallions are obnoxious creatures —always kicking, biting, and fighting among themselves.

Sex Determination — Very difficult to determine and the reason why most hunting permits do not specify the sex to be taken. Stallions and mares have similar pattern configurations and a similar body size and weight. A stallion's neck is thicker and the head larger compared to overall body size. Behavior in the herd important: When spooked, a family group will always be led away by mare; stallion follows at the rear and often stops to look back. When a herd approaches water, stallion will always lead. When the herd is feeding peacefully or resting, the stallion will usually be on the periphery. Stallion has more brown (shadow stripes) between stripes.

Trophy Assessment — For trophies, old stallions usually have scarred/damaged, lower-quality hides while young bachelor-herd stallions have the best skins, a fact that makes them the targets of choice. For baiting purposes, any stallion or old, barren mare will do.

Zebra

The Hunt — Zebras are most active during the early morning and late afternoon. They are nonterritorial but have home ranges. These frequent and regular drinkers prefer clean, clear water and rarely venture far from this source. Usually drink at night. Donkeylike spoor distinctive and easy to follow. Find fresh spoor at a water source and follow it, or glass all likely areas of suitable habitat. In mountainous areas, glass from elevated point at first light.

Rifle, Caliber, and Bullet Selection — Zebras require a minimum caliber/bullet combination in the .270-, 7mm-, or .30-caliber range and controlled-expansion softpoint bullets of at least 150 grains in weight. On this really tough species, larger calibers and heavier bullets are more effective: the .338s and 250-grainers are a good choice. An alternative to this is the 9.3mms and .375s with good 250- to 300-grainers.

Shot Placement — High heart/lung shot most recommended because it's the largest target area with most room for shot-placement error. Sight up center line of front leg and place shot on that line somewhere between one-third and halfway up body. Body stripes usually split into an inverted "Y" (λ) in this area, and this makes for a good aiming point. High shoulder/spinal shot will drop a zebra. Place shot higher up and farther forward on shoulder, through center of shoulder blade. Spine/neck shot: Place shot in middle of neck where it joins body.

Zebra

Zebra

Center of "vital triangle," high heart/lung shot most effective and best option. High shoulder/spinal will drop a sable.

SABLE
Hippotragus niger

Natural History — This impressive and sought-after trophy animal has distinctive white facial and belly markings and a black coat, the reason for its common name. It has heavily ridged, backward-sweeping horns. Aggressive and bold, the sable will not hesitate to charge if wounded, cornered, or simply threatened. Gregarious herd animals. Master bull dominates a herd, but oldest and wisest cow leads it. Frequent drinkers with territory near permanent source of water. Selective grazing animals. Three subspecies recognized.

Sex Determination — Both sexes carry horns, but those of trophy bulls are considerably thicker, more heavily ridged, and sweepingly curved. Mature bulls are pitch black with a distinctly white underbelly. Cows darken with age but retain a dull rusty red tinge; cows have thinner, straighter horns.

Trophy Assessment — Trophy quality can properly be assessed only from the side-on position. Look for good vertical height, extended tips, and thick bases. Horn length of 40 inches or more is considered good for common sable while horns of 44+ are really good and those of 48 or more inches are exceptional. Horns on giant sable can reach 60 inches long. Good bases = 10 inches. SCI method (1): length of both horns + circumference of both horns at bases. RW method (7): length of longest horn.

The Hunt — Most active during the early morning and late afternoon; likes to graze in or near open grasslands. This water-dependent species is encountered in areas of suitable habitat near water. Look for arrowhead-shaped spoor in the vicinity of watering points. Catch sable at first light while they are still out feeding in an open, short-grass area, or in a recently burned-off area. Herd bull will usually be somewhere on the periphery. This proud and aloof antelope is not all that difficult to approach. Can be aggressive when wounded.

Rifle, Caliber, and Bullet Selection — Sables are a heavy, tough, and potentially aggressive antelope. Do not be undergunned. While the legal minimum is the .270, the .30-06 or .300 Winchester Magnum and 200- or 220-grain controlled-expansion softpoints are more sensible options. An even better choice is the .338 with 250-grain bullets as well as the 9.3mms or .375s.

Shot Placement — Be careful not to damage trophy or cape. The side-on high heart/lung shot is the best option as it gives the largest margin for shot-placement error and is the most effective. Place shot through center of "vital triangle." The high shoulder/spinal shot is more specialized and should be placed through the shoulder blade. This will drop a sable.

Side-on anatomy diagram.

Roan

The center of the vital triangle, a high heart/lung shot, is the best shot placement option from side-on.

ROAN

Hippotragus equinus

Natural History — The roan antelope is one of Africa's glamour species. It is Africa's second largest antelope, with mature bulls weighing as much as 600 pounds. It has long, sideways-pointing, tip-tufted ears, and it is strawberry roan or pink grayish-brown. This selective, long-grass grazer favors open savanna grasslands and especially likes thick, tall, sweet palatable grasses and open bushveld; it browses occasionally. It is a regular drinker that needs permanent access to clean, open surface water. As a diurnal species, it feeds most actively during the cooler daylight hours. Naturally nervous, it prefers its own company. Semigregarious, it will be found in small breeding herds.

Sex Determination — Both sexes carry ridged, rearward-facing sweeping horns. Those of mature bulls are thicker and sturdier than those of cows. Because bulls are a lot bigger and more heavily set than females, sex determination is easy, even from a distance.

Trophy Assessment — Judging length is relatively easy and is best done from the front. Length of the face from the horn bases to tip of the nostril is the reference length. Horns that stick up above the head to a height equal to the length of the face will be in the 25- to 26-inch range. One-and-a-quarter times the length of the face = 28 inches; one-and-a-half times = more than 30 inches and is an exceptional trophy. Good bases = 8 to 9 inches. SCI Method (1): RW method (7)

The Perfect Shot: Mini Edition for Africa II

The Hunt — While it is not a difficult species to hunt, it is not an overly abundant species. Easy to spot from a distance. Roans have home ranges, so they remain in an area and are easier to find a second time. Best trophies are old, displaced, post-breeding-age males; such bulls are nomadic. Chance encounters require luck. Roans are easier to hunt on game ranches because a specific post-breeding bull will be identified by the owner. Roans are water-dependent and drink daily. Find distinctive spoor and track. Most are spotted from a hunting vehicle and then stalked.

Rifle, Caliber, and Bullet Selection — Various 7mms and good-quality 175-grainers are the minimum. The .30s and 200- or 220-grainers are better. The .338 Winchester Magnum and good 250-grainers, or the .358s and 275-grainers are about ideal. The 9.3mms or even the .375s with 250-, 260-, 270-, or even 300-grainers are the best choice. It is an open-country species, so shooting distances can be long. A good scope is essential.

Shot Placement — The top of the heart/center of the lungs shot is the one recommended. Because it is an open-country species, take time to place shot perfectly. Get into the right position and wait for a perfectly positioned shooting opportunity. From a side-on position, the vital triangle shot is always the best option. Another option is the high shoulder/spinal shot; this shot will drop a roan. On quartering shots, it's necessary to get the angles right; bisect the space created by the front legs.

Side-on anatomy diagram.

The high heart/lung shot is always the best option from side-on.

Waterbuck

WATERBUCK
Kobus ellipsiprymnus

Natural History — Terrible to eat but stately to look at. The waterbuck has a high water requirement, so it is a regular and frequent drinker and can usually be encountered near some form of water. Has oily skin. White markings on rump (defassa group has solid white rump patch; ringed or common group has large white ring). Gregarious herd animals. Life expectancy is up to 15 years. Predominantly grazers. Up to six waterbuck subspecies recognized.

Sex Determination — Only waterbuck bulls have horns, so sex determination is easy. The horns of a really good trophy bull are large, impressive, and easy to identify.

Trophy Assessment — Horns can only be properly assessed from the front: Length, degree of divergence, and thickness of bases are all easy to see and evaluate from this angle. From side, look for forward curvature, which adds to score. Look for bulls with the high-scoring combination of good horn length, horn symmetry, and thick, heavy bases (8 to 11 inches). A good head is 29 inches; a very good head is 30 inches; and anything over 31 inches is superb. SCI method (1): add the length of both horns + circumference of both horns at bases. RW method (7): length of longest horn.

Waterbuck

The Hunt — Mature bulls are territorial. They like open grasslands and flood plains near large stretches of water. Even though they have good eyesight and hearing, they are not all that difficult to approach. A good binocular is essential to evaluate trophy quality from a distance. They can also be encountered in thickly bushed areas where they can be elusive and a challenge to hunt.

Rifle, Caliber, and Bullet Selection — Trophy waterbucks weigh 550 to 600 pounds. For open grassland conditions, the .270s and 150-grain softpoint bullets are as small a caliber and as light a bullet that can be recommended; the various 7mms and .30 calibers with good 175- to 220-grain controlled-expansion softpoints offer a better, more effective option, especially for "bush" areas. Larger calibers and heavier bullets are even more effective.

Shot Placement — A shoulder mount is the best way to display waterbuck; consequently, avoid neck shots that could ruin cape. The high heart/lung shot is recommended: Sight up the front leg and place the shot on that line, somewhere between one-third and halfway up the body. Shoulder/spinal shot: Place higher up on shoulder, above the body's horizontal midline and farther forward, through the middle of the shoulder blade. In open country, a high, behind-the-shoulder lung shot is also effective.

The Perfect Shot: Mini Edition for Africa II

Side-on anatomy diagram.

Waterbuck

The high heart/lung shot is the most effective option from side-on.

Blue Wildebeest

BLUE WILDEBEEST
Connochaetes taurinus (brindled)

Natural History — Even though the direct translation of wildebeest means "wild ox," it is a member of the antelope family. It is a strange and ugly creature with a reputation for incredible toughness. Also known as the "poor man's buffalo." These gregarious herd animals may be in herds of many thousands when migrating. They are exclusively short-grass grazers. They are often encountered with other grazers like zebra. Four subspecies recognized.

Sex Determination — Not easy to distinguish. Both sexes have horns and are similar in body size and color. Breeding bulls have deeper bodies and are more masculine looking. Older bulls are darker with more and wider stripes on their sides; their foreheads and muzzles are pitch black with no trace of brown. Horn bases are thick and well developed; horns may droop slightly to just below level of the extended ear tips before curling upward. During the rut, tree bark stain appears on horns near bases.

Trophy Assessment — Can be properly assessed only from the front. Look for big, easily visible bosses (12 to 15 inches in circumference) and a horn spread greater than the width of the extended ear tips. If so, it equals 24 inches and is a respectable trophy. The wider the spread, the better. It's important to assess a trophy bull's mane and beard for shoulder mount. Old bulls will have blunt, worn-down tips that can make for interesting trophies. SCI method (5) for common wildebeest: tip-to-tip measurement of horns + circumference

Blue Wildebeest

of bosses of both horns. RW method (12) for common wildebeest: outside spread + inside spread + length of longest horn + width of wider boss.

The Hunt — On plains and in open spaces, the wildebeest is easy to locate from a distance, but in bushveld conditions, it's more difficult. The wildebeest can be elusive and shy. In sandy, sparsely grassy areas, they can be hunted by tracking (splayed toes, deeply imprinted forefeet spoor). Productive hunting method is to walk slowly through likely resting areas, into or across the wind. Stop frequently and glass well ahead; look for movement and then stalk closer.

Rifle, Caliber, and Bullet Selection — The wildebeest is a remarkably tough antelope. For open terrain hunting, the .270s and good 150-grain bullets are the minimum recommendation; 7mms with 175-grain bullets and .30s with 200- or 220-grain bullets are a better option. Even larger calibers—all the way up to the .40s—are recommended for short-range "bushveld" conditions.

Shot Placement — Prominent hump on shoulders and long mane hairs can lead to body shots being placed too high. The side-on, high heart/lung shot is recommended as it has the largest margin for shot-placement error. Come up back edge of the front leg and place the shot above the point of the elbow joint just below the body's horizontal midline.

Blue Wildebeest

Blue Wildebeest

Perfect shot presents themselves—just ensure that the bullets end up in, or passes through, the chest cavity.

BONGO
Tragelaphus eurycerus eurycerus

Natural History — The bongo belongs to the striped, spiral-horned antelope family and is one of the world's premier trophies. This rare antelope can weigh up to 900 pounds and is large in body size. The bongo has a rich, reddish-tan color and a body shape similar to the bushbuck's. This shy, elusive, and wary antelope is a mixed feeder that lives in the rain forests of West and Central Africa. The bongo likes natural salt licks and can be found in small family groups, as solitary individuals, or as small groups of bulls. Can be aggressive when cornered or threatened.

Sex Determination — In rain forests where visibility is restricted, it is never easy to get a good view of quarry, so sex determination can be difficult. Both sexes carry horns, so be careful not to shoot a female. While the shape of the horns is similar, male horns are thicker and heavier. Likewise, mature males are heavier set and more muscular. Cow horns are thinner, shorter, and sometimes misshapen. A lone animal can be a female, so be very sure of sex before shooting. Size of spoor useful in determining sex as bulls have bigger tracks.

Trophy Assessment — Important to view horns from the front and the side. Look for a bull with horn mass, a big bell, long tips that kick outward to form a lyre shape, and thick, heavy bases. Horns of 27 inches are good, 28 to 30 inches are very good, 30 to 32 inches are excellent, and above 32 inches is exceptional. Good bases will be 9 to 11 inches in circumference. SCI method (2): RW method (8)

The Hunt — Three ways to hunt bongo include track, walk, and stalk; with dogs; and from a machan. The walk, track, and stalk method is the most challenging, and success is never guaranteed. Rain is essential to track successfully. Dogs dramatically increase chances of success. The bongo is aggressive and bays easily; that offers more time to assess trophy. Machan sitting offers good shooting rest and time to assess trophy carefully. Don't stay in machan too long—three days is the maximum before changing position.

Rifle, Caliber, and Bullet Selection — Because bongos live in thick rain forest, the hunter usually has to shoot through vegetation. Bongos are also large and aggressive. Any of the .375s and good quality 300-grain expanding bullets are a sensible choice. A low-power or red-dot scope is essential as light is poor in the bongo's habitat. Because other dangerous species also occur in the rain forests, it is better to be over- than undergunned. A .400 double makes good sense. Environmental conditions are such that a rifle will get wet and rust.

Shot Placement — Due to hunting circumstances, perfect shot placement is never guaranteed. Take whatever shot presents itself, which is the reason large calibers and heavy bullets are recommended as they are effective from all angles. From whatever angle, place shot so that bullet lands up in, or passes through, the chest cavity.

Side-on anatomy diagram.

Oryx/Gemsbok

High heart/lung shot always best in open country because it offers the greatest margin for shot-placement error.

ORYX / GEMSBOK
Oryx gazella

Natural History — Known as the "desert warrior." Gemsbok are courageous; they are extremely aggressive and dangerous when cornered, injured, or threatened. Primarily a dry, open-country species, they thrive in hot, waterless expanses. Can survive without surface drinking water for many months. Gemsbok are grazers but will also browse if necessary. Gregarious herd animals. Four subspecies recognized.

Sex Determination — Both sexes carry horns. Horns of mature females are usually longer and thinner, bases are less massive, horns may curve rearward slightly, and horns are often deformed. A bull's horns are thicker, straighter, and more "V" shaped. Distance between bases is greater on males than females.

Trophy Assessment — Trophies of either sex are eligible for record-book entry. Females often outscore males because horns are usually longer. A gemsbok's head is 18 inches in length, so two-and-a-quarter times the length of head will equal 40-inch horns, the gemsbok holy grail. Good bases on males should be 8 to 9 inches around while good bases on cows are 6 to 7 inches. SCI method (1): length of both horns + circumference of both horns at bases. RW method (7): length of longest horn.

The Hunt — Open country gemsboks are wary, and their good eyesight makes getting close difficult. Need good binocular so as to be able to judge trophy quality from a distance. Flat-shooting caliber/cartridge combination essential as shooting distances are usually far. A rangefinder is very useful. Bushveld conditions are very different, and the hunt will be one of walk, spot, and stalk. Shooting distances much shorter. In such conditions gemsbok can be wary, spooky, and elusive.

Rifle, Caliber, and Bullet Selection — For wide-open spaces, flat-shooters with a scope are absolutely essential. A minimum of .270 and good 150-grainers is necessary. Hot 7mms or .30s with 175- to 200-grain bullets are better. The best option is the .338 and 225- or 250-grain bullets. Bushveld conditions make for shorter shooting distances, and there a 7mm Mauser and good 175-grain softpoints are a sensible minimum.

Shot Placement — This is a tough and aggressive animal, so make the first shot count. There is a tendency to shoot too high; never shoot above horizontal midline. Side-on high heart/lung shot always the best option with greatest margin for shot-placement error, especially at long range. Bushveld conditions offer other options: shoulder/spinal or upper neck/spinal at base of skull. Because this is one of best-eating antelope, neck or brain shots are an option for the meat/biltong hunter.

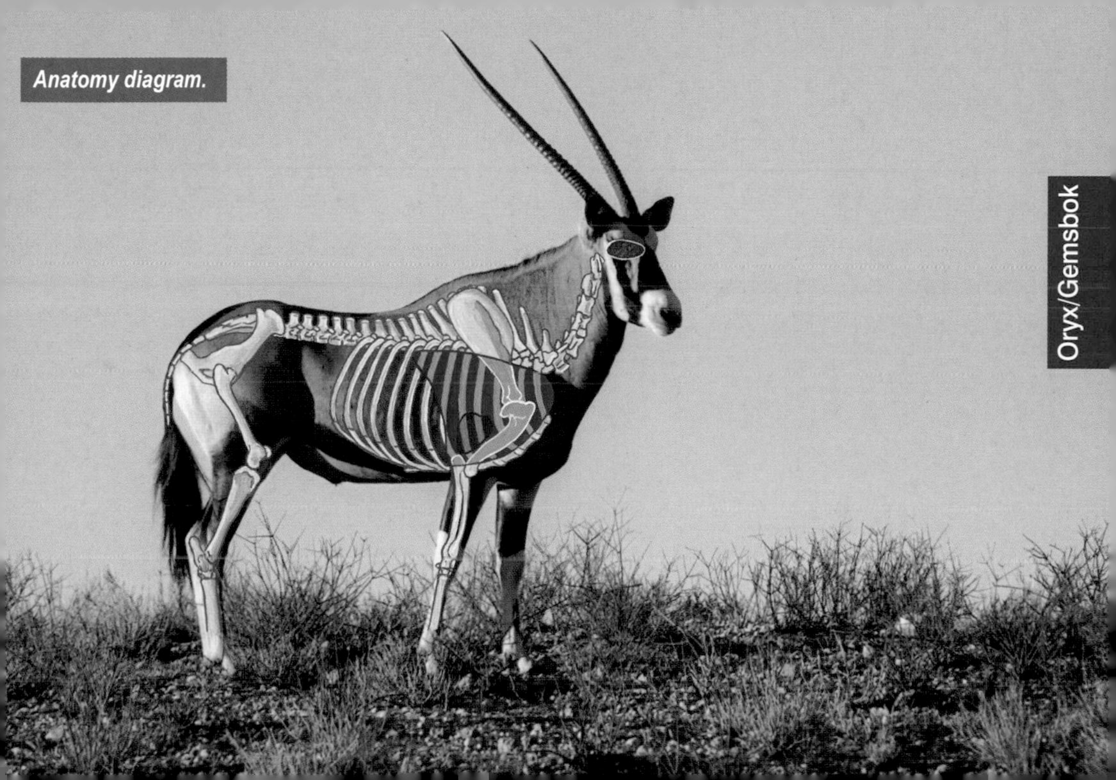

Hartebeest

The center of the vital triangle and the top of the heart is just below the horizontal midline and just above the line of the vertical front leg.

HARTEBEEST
Alcelaphus spp.

Natural History — Hartebeests have long, narrow heads; yellow goatlike eyes; slender necks; long, pointed ears; prominently high withers; a sloping backline; matchstick legs; and relatively unimpressive horns. These very fleet antelopes have legendary endurance. Horns originate at the very top of the head from a pedicel. These gregarious herd animals are primarily grazers that prefer open grasslands, *vlei* areas, and semidesert bush savanna. They feed during cooler times of day and drink when water is available but can go without. Up to nine subspecies.

Sex Determination — Mature males are more robustly built and generally darker in color. Both male and female carry heavily ringed horns. Horn bases of mature bulls considerably thicker and more massive than those of females, and in open country it's possible to see the penis button.

Trophy Assessment — Essential to evaluate from both the frontal and side-on positions. Look for thick bases, good vertical height, and long angled tips. SCI method (1): length of both horns + circumference of both horns at bases. RW method (7): length of longest horn.

The Hunt — Easy to locate in open country. Glass from an elevated vantage point and also check salt pans and mineral licks. Ambush a herd arriving at or leaving a shady resting place. Hartebeests have good hearing and an acute sense of smell, but their eyesight is not all that good. They are vulnerable to a stalk at first or last light. They are not particularly difficult to hunt; meat quality considered poor.

Rifle, Caliber, and Bullet Selection — A relatively flat-shooting caliber is necessary as shots are usually long. The .270s and quality 130-grain expanding bullets are a sensible minimum. The various 7mms and 140- to 160-grain bullets of good ballistic coefficient are probably better. The .308 Winchester and .30-06 with bullets in the 165-grain weight range are also suitable if sighted in appropriately for the expected longer-than-usual shooting distances.

Shot Placement — Humped withers often cause hunters to shoot too high. A side-on, high heart/lung shot is recommended because it is most effective and there is a good margin for placement error. Place your shot no higher than body's horizontal midline on line of front leg. At long range, a high, behind-the-shoulder lung shot is also effective as it, too, has a good margin for shot-placement error. Shots placed a little too far behind will hit the liver.

Side-on anatomy diagram.

Hartebeest

At long range, the high heart/lung shot placement option offers the largest margin for shot-placement error.

BLACK WILDEBEEST
Connochaetes gnou

Natural History — Also known as "white tailed gnu," wildebeests are often called "the clowns of the veld." This species is found only in parts of South Africa, Botswana, and Namibia. It is considered to be one of Africa's odd-ball antelope species. Mature bulls are stocky in appearance but appear bigger than they really are. They are so ugly they are almost beautiful. They live in open country and are short-grass grazers. They occur in breeding herds of 20 to 60 animals, but bachelor herds and lone bulls also occur. Mature males are territorial during the March/May rutting season. They are active during the early morning and late afternoon in the open environments they prefer. These regular drinkers seek water usually late in the afternoon. This is a popular and exclusively Southern African trophy species.

Sex Determination — Both sexes carry odd-shaped, forward-pointing, and upward-lifting horns. This makes sex determination difficult. Always check the ventral bodyline. The penis button can usually be seen. Mature bulls are more muscular in the neck and shoulder region, stand taller than cows, and have heavier, better developed bosses. Male horns are always thicker and more massive, which is easy to see from a distance. A lone animal will be a territorial bull. A good binocular is essential for sex determination and trophy assessment.

Trophy Assessment — One of the more difficult species to evaluate because it is usually done at great distance. Old bulls with well-developed bosses are the best trophies. From side-on position, look for horn drop to below eye level before rising vertically to or above the level of the top of the boss. Horn tips that stick up a couple of inches above boss level will usually make the book. SCI method (6): RW method (13)

The Hunt — This can be difficult due to open terrain, and the spot, walk, and stalk method can be a real challenge because they never stand still. This naturally cautious species has good eyesight, and they always keep a 250-pace "comfort zone" around themselves. Sometimes curious, they will approach suspicious objects. Long shots are the norm.

Rifle, Caliber, and Bullet Selection — For their size, they are an exceptionally tough species, so use .270s and good, high BC 130- or 150-grainers as a sensible minimum. Hotter 7mms like the 7x64mm, the 7mm Remington Magnum, or the .280 Ackley with quality, high BC 160- or 175-grainers are better. The .30 cartridges with 180s are also good options when sighted in for long-range shooting. A rangefinder, shooting rest, and a good scope are essential.

Shot Placement — The only recommended shot-placement option is the one that offers the greatest margin for shot-placement error, and that is the high heart/lung shot. Place the shot on the line of the front leg at the shoulder joint. The hunter needs patience for the wildebeest to stand still and to be perfectly side-on.

The Perfect Shot: Mini Edition for Africa II

Side-on anatomy diagram.

Black Wildebeest

Take whatever shot presents itself. Just be sure the bullet will pass through the chest cavity. As indicated, from side-on, the high heart/lung shot is always the best option.

NYALA
Tragelaphus angasii

Natural History — This Southern African species is often considered the most beautiful of the striped, spiral-horned antelope. It is also unique and affordable. The nyala is cousin to the bushbuck, bongo, and kudu. At 250 pounds, the nyala is a medium-size antelope. It has a narrow body and slab sides. The nyala is perfectly adapted to thick bushy areas. It is a mixed feeder that favors wetlands and open grasslands. Nyalas are encountered in small family or breeding units. Mature, trophy-size bulls are usually loners. Small bachelor herds also occur. They are not territorial but do occupy home ranges.

Sex Determination — Mature bulls are dark gray with distinct yellow legs. Only males carry horns, which are more twisted than spiral. Ewes are heavily striped and are a distinct rusty, orange brown.

Trophy Assessment — This is one of the easier species to judge. From the front, horns have a "bell" shape. The size of the "bell" and the direction of the horn tips indicate both trophy quality and size. Distinct bell and inward-pointing horn tips = 22 inches. A good bell has tips that go straight upward = 24 inches. Tips that diverge out = 26 inches. Best trophies have thick bases, a good "bell," and outward-flaring, ivory-capped tips. Good bases = 8 to 9 inches. SCI method (2); RW method (8).

The Hunt — Nyalas are naturally cautious and have refined senses. The most successful hunting method is by walk-and-stalk, into or across the prevailing wind, through suitably thick habitat. Ambushing likely feeding areas at first or last light can also be productive. A good scope is essential. Because of the thick cover, shots are usually taken at close range.

Rifle, Caliber, and Bullet Selection — Nyalas are neither tough nor tenacious. An ideal nyala combination is the 7x57mm and roundnose and 175-grain softpoints. Alternative good options include 7mm-08 and 160-grainers, .308 Winchester and 180-grainers, or .30-06 with 200s.

Shot Placement — The hunter usually has to take whatever shot presents itself . . . and do it quickly. The bullet needs to pass through or end up in the "boiler room." The top-of-heart/center-of-lungs shot is always the most effective, no matter from which angle the shooter is.

Side-on anatomy diagram.

The "vital triangle" and high "behind-the-shoulder" lung shots are indicated.

Reedbuck

REEDBUCK
Redunca spp.

Natural History — The common reedbuck is a widely distributed species that likes open grassland, marshy areas, flood plains, and reedbeds. It is a graceful, medium-size, 180-pound antelope. Mountain reedbucks are found in completely different habitats. They are a smaller, delicate, 60-pound antelope that favors rocky, broken, hilly country. Both types of reedbucks are exclusively grazers that drink frequently.

Sex Determination — Only reedbuck rams have horns, and these curve sharply forward. The horns are cross-ringed.

Trophy Assessment — This is one of the easier species to assess, and it is easy to see horn length from a distance. SCI method (1B)—only the length of each horn is combined for a total score. Base measurements are omitted because of the soft and pulpy bases. RW method (7): Mountain reedbuck horns shorter and thicker. Use ears for length reference.

The Hunt — Each reedbuck type requires its own hunting technique. Look for habitat suitable to the species being hunted. Early morning and late afternoon are the best hunting times. This is when reedbucks are most active and on their way either to or from feeding grounds. They lie up during heat of day. Because they often stop to look back after running off, this provides a shooting opportunity, so be ready for it. Mountain reedbucks are best hunted from above by spotting and stalking. Reedbucks are territorial, so the hunter can usually find an animal again if initially unsuccessful. They are extremely good to eat.

Rifle, Caliber, and Bullet Selection — Reedbucks are neither tough nor tenacious. They are easily killed with expanding bullets in the 80- to 100-grain-weight range. The 6mms or .243 offers a good starting point. Also try the .25-06 with 115 or 120 grains. Larger calibers cause less meat damage, and these include the .270s, 7mms, or even the .30s with 130- to 180-grain bullets. A good scope is essential.

Shot Placement — Reedbucks drop easily with shots placed into the heart/lung area. The vital triangle shot is always the best, most effective option with the greatest margin for shot-placement error. A behind-the-shoulder, high lung shot is less wasteful for the meat for the biltong hunter.

Reedbuck

Side-on anatomy diagram.

All the shot-placement options are indicated: high lung, high heart/lung, upper neck/spinal, and brain shot.

Blesbok

BLESBOK / BONTEBOK
Damaliscus dorcas phillipsi / D. d. dorcas

Natural History — Blesboks and bonteboks are both medium-size South African antelopes. The blesbok is one of the more common species on many South African game ranches, considered a "bread-and-butter" species. It is one of the easier species to harvest. White blesboks also occur and are easy to see from a distance. Bonteboks have never learned to be "wary" and are, therefore, easy to hunt. These two races are exclusively grazers, preferring short grass. They are most active early morning and late afternoon. They drink daily, are a gregarious species, and favor open, expansive areas. Both occur in breeding herds, as individual territorial rams, and in bachelor herds. They are seasonal breeders, and their eyesight is excellent.

Sex Determination — Both sexes carry horns. Those of mature blesbok rams are considerably thicker with prominent, easily visible, straw-colored cross ridges. Males have a penis button and yellow-stained white muzzles. Mature, trophy-size rams are strongly territorial, are encountered as loners, and can be found at the periphery of herds. Ewes will be in herds, and their horns are thinner.

Trophy Assessment — A good binocular is necessary. Horns that are the length of face will be 15 to 16 inches long and a good trophy. High-scoring blesboks often have horns with points that diverge outward. Good bases will be 6½ inches around. Blesbok's ears are 6 inches in length. Horns twice the ear length will be a good trophy. Compare the overall length of the horns to that of the blesbok's face to estimate length of horns. SCI method (1) RW method (8).

The Hunt — Depending on the hunting pressure, hunts will either be too easy or a real challenge. Habitat is in open country, so shots tend to be long. Easy to spot from a distance, and as they tend to stay in same areas, they are easy to locate a second time. Ambush such sites. This inquisitive species will come closer when suspicious. Good optics are essential.

Rifle, Caliber, and Bullet Selection — Blesboks are easily killed with good quality 80- to 100-grain bullets. The .243 Winchester is a popular choice. The .25-06 and good 115- or 120-grainers are better. So are the .270 Winchester and 130s or 150s or the 7mms and .30s with 165- to 180-grain expanding bullets.

Shot Placement — Shooting distances are usually long, so take the shot that offers the greatest margin for shot-placement error: high heart/lung shot, through the center of the vital triangle—although this shot can be wasteful if the hunter wants to use the meat. For meat or biltong hunters, place shot "just behind the shoulder for a high lung shot." For long range, only side-on shots should be taken. When culling, the head and upper neck shots are the best as this is the least wasteful of meat.

The Perfect Shot: Mini Edition for Africa II

Side-on anatomy diagram.

Blesbok

A high, behind-the-shoulder lung shot is effective for the meat-conscious biltong hunter.

Impala

IMPALA

Aepyceros melampus

Natural History — Impalas are commonly used as camp meat and as bait for leopards, are good for "cutting hunting teeth" on, and are considered a "bread-and-butter" species. They have lyre-shape horns and two oval, raised, black-hair scent glands on the inside of their hind legs, above the hoof. These gregarious herd animals both graze and browse; they prefer open, heavily grazed, almost barren areas adjacent to or within open woodland, bushveld, or mopane scrub. They never venture far from water and they must drink at least once daily. Impalas have superb eyesight, hearing, and sense of smell. Three subspecies recognized.

Sex Determination — Only rams have horns, but the impala's propensity to clump together in thick bush makes it difficult to tell the difference.

Trophy Assessment — Look for horns with long, smooth, and sharply pointed tips; also look for tips that point vertically and are parallel with each other or diverge outward. Good bases and a length of 21 inches should make the SCI book. SCI method (1): length of both horns + circumference of both horns at bases. RW method (7): length of longest horn.

The Hunt — During autumn rut and wintertime hunting season, the best rams are usually found with breeding herds. Most active during the cooler times of the day. Ambush known feeding areas. When

Impala

alarmed, impala will bunch together, making it easy to accidentally shoot more than one with a single shot. Be careful of this.

Rifle, Caliber, and Bullet Selection — Although the .22 centerfires are legal, they are not recommended. The 6mms (.243s.) are much more effective. The 7x57mm with 175-grain roundnose softpoints has a wonderful reputation for bushveld conditions. The .308 Winchester or the .30-06 with 180-grain softpoints are also a good choice. A good scope is essential for precise shot placement.

Shot Placement — Impalas are tough for their size. High heart/lung shot recommended: Place into center of "vital triangle." A high, behind-the-shoulder lung shot is less likely to spoil "good-eating" meat. From the side-on position, place just behind shoulder and directly above elbow, where fawn-color hide changes to a rusty brick-brownish-orange. Head and neck shots are a lot more difficult and only for the experienced hunter. These shots are the domain of the professional "culler" or meat hunter.

Impala

The Perfect Shot: Mini Edition for Africa II

Side-on anatomy diagram.

Impala

Bushbucks are aggressive. The recommended shot is to the shoulder/spinal area (top), which will produce a "drop-to-the-shot" effect. The high heart/lung shot (bottom) is also indicated.

BUSHBUCK
Tragelaphus scriptus

Natural History — Bushbucks are challenging to hunt because they are shy and elusive. Subspecies vary widely in color, pattern, and extent of stripes, chevrons, blazes, and dots. Body and horn size can also vary considerably; they weigh 80 to 140 pounds. They are solitary animals, including trophy-size rams. They have distinct home ranges and like thick bush in riverine areas. They are almost exclusively browsers. Life expectancy is about 12 years. The alarm signal is a doglike bark. Up to nine subspecies recognized.

Sex Determination — Only male bushbucks carry horns. Mature males are considerably larger, stockier, and generally darker overall than the females. Males are chestnut brown to almost black while females are light brown to fawn.

Trophy Assessment — Relatively easy to assess from the front. Thickness of horns and visible length influence whether trophy scores will be high. Horn tips usually point upward, parallel to each other. Even better are horn tips that diverge outward. Good bases are 5 to 7 inches. SCI method (2): length of horns around spiral ridge + circumference of both horns at bases. RW method (8): length of longest horn measured around spiral.

The Hunt — Often likened to hunting the American white-tailed deer. Look for suitable habitat, including areas of thick vegetation bordering rivers. Still-hunting through suitable habitat is one of the most productive hunting methods. Walk into or across the wind, moving quietly, stopping frequently to probe the densest cover. Wounded bushbuck are aggressive and will not hesitate to charge. Bushbucks are often hunted in dangerous-game country.

Rifle, Caliber, and Bullet Selection — The 7x57mm, .308 Winchester, or .30-06 and suitable 175-, 180-, and 220-grain bullets are sensible minimums for bushbuck. It's important to be suitably armed for any eventuality in dangerous-game country.

Shot Placement — Care should be taken to avoid damaging either cape or horns. From any angle, place the shot so that the bullet gets into or passes through the chest cavity.

Side-on anatomy diagram.

All the shot-placement options are indicated: brain, upper neck/spinal, high heart/lung and high, behind-the-shoulder lung shot.

Springbok

SPRINGBOK
Antidorcas marsupialis

Natural History — The springbok is the national emblem of South Africa; the name means "jump buck" and is derived from their behavior of *stotting* , a pogo-stick style of jumping when alarmed. Exclusively a Southern African species. Weight varies by subspecies with mature males weighing 75 to 100 pounds. Gregarious herd animals of dry, open grassland and semidesert. They are both grazers and browsers, preferring short-grass terrain with stunted semidesert shrubs and bushes. Not dependent on water but will drink when water is available. Up to three subspecies and two color phases recognized. It is an important South African and Namibian game-ranch animal.

Sex Determination — Both sexes carry horns. Those of the female are thinner, spindlier-looking, straighter, more upright, and less curved. Tips are usually bent, pointing inward toward each other. Horns of trophy-quality rams longer, more obviously curved, considerably thicker and more massive, and more conspicuously ridged. The older a male gets, the more rearward-pointing the tips will become; really good trophies have "meathook"-shape, rearward-pointing tips. Although of similar size, mature females are also generally lighter in weight.

Trophy Assessment — Because horns are relatively small and because it's hard to get close enough to evaluate the springbok, it's difficult to judge trophy quality. Base thickness and overall length are important;

curves will be more angular on good specimens. Main body of the horns are splayed. Look for vertical horn length twice that of erect ears. Good bases will be 6 inches, and 13- to 14-inch horns should make the SCI record book. SCI method (1): length of both horns + circumference of both horns at bases. RW method (7): length of longest horn.

The Hunt — Because it's renowned as the best-eating of all African antelopes, demand for springbok meat is high. Harvested on game farms through rifle culling. The springbok presents a great challenge to hunt "fair chase" in the wild. Springboks have phenomenal eyesight and they are naturally paranoid about being approached; thus, they are challenging to hunt by sight-and-stalk methods. Be prepared for much walking and crawling. Ambush known feeding areas like fringes of pans or physical barriers like fence lines. Shooting distances of up to 300 paces are normal.

Rifle, Caliber, and Bullet Selection — Flat-shooters are essential as shots out to 300 paces are common and areas are often windy. Choose calibers capable of firing bullets of at least 120 grains, at muzzle velocities in excess of 2,600 fps. The .25-06, the various 6.5mms, the .264 Winchester, the .270s, and the various 7mms are all good choices. A good scope is essential for such long shots.

Shot Placement — A side-on lung shot (just behind shoulder) is the shot of choice for the meat hunter. Side-on high heart/lung shot recommended for the trophy hunter. Head and upper-neck shots are recommended only for the professional "culler."

Springbok

The barrel roundness of a warthog makes identifying the vital triangle difficult. Sight up from the line of the vertical front leg to place the shot just below the horizontal midline. This will be the top of the heart.

Warthog

WARTHOG
Phacochoerus aethiopicus

Natural History — This distant cousin of the European boar is popular with Continental safari clients. It is ugly to the point of being lovable. The warthog is hunted for its tusks, hide, and as a trophy. It is one of the better-tasting game meats and a good bait for leopard. A warthog can weigh as much as 250 pounds and is one of the toughest of all African species. Warthogs are active during daylight and spend their nights in unused antbear burrows. They are almost exclusively grazers. Not territorial, they wander wherever food supply dictates. They love to wallow in mud and take dust baths. While not entirely water dependent, they will drink regularly when water is available. Frequently encountered near wet, marshy areas. Their habit of rooting with their snouts disturbs large areas of habitat. They occur in small family groups or "sounders."

Sex Determination — Warthogs get their name from their facial "warts." All warthogs have a pair of warts; males have a second pair on the side of the muzzle just above the upper tusks. The testicles on a mature boar are easily visible. Mature boars are considerably larger and more massive than sows, with bigger, longer, and thicker tusks.

Trophy Assessment — Warthogs have two sets of tusks, but only the larger upper-jaw pair is measured. Tusks are easily visible, but from one-third to as much as one-half is embedded in the skull. Look for tusks with good visible thickness and length. Average tusk circumference is 5 inches. Those that stick out 7 inches should make the SCI record book. SCI method (12): length of both tusks + circumference of both tusks at largest place. RW method (6): length of longest tusk.

The Hunt — Search for suitable feeding grounds (pans, marshy areas, recently burned-off *vleis*). Warthogs feed throughout the day. Their eyes are close to the ground, so they do not see well; however, they have excellent hearing and a good sense of smell. Approach slowly from downwind. Ambush them in a mud wallow.

Rifle, Caliber, and Bullet Selection — The various 7mms and the .30 calibers with quality 160- to 180-grain softpoint bullets are a good choice. On big, trophy-size boars, larger calibers and heavier bullets are more effective. Warthogs are often hunted in dangerous-game areas, so be prepared for any eventuality. It's better to be overgunned for a warthog than undergunned for something dangerous.

Shot Placement — The barrel roundness of a big trophy boar, its long mane hairs, and the apparent absence of a neck can make shot placement challenging. A side-on, high heart/lung shot is the most effective: Sight up center line of front leg and place the shot just below body's horizontal midline.

Warthog

Duiker

The high shoulder/spinal shot will drop a duiker; the high heart/lung one may not.

BUSH DUIKER
Subfamily Cephalophus

Natural History — The species varies greatly in weight, from less than 9 to more than 175 pounds. Bush duikers need bush for browse and for protection, giving rise to their common name. Forest duikers found in wet, lush rain forest. Duikers are solitary antelopes, most often encountered alone; they are fertile and prolific breeders. Most active during the late afternoon and early evening, but become nocturnal when subjected to intensive hunting pressure. They have an extremely varied diet; they are primarily browsers, but will feed on other foodstuffs not usually considered antelope food. Able to survive in proximity to man. They are not dependent on water, for they get sufficient moisture from their varied diet. Four subspecies of bush duiker and up to twenty species of forest duiker recognized.

Sex Determination — Only male bush duikers have horns. A few females carry horns, but these are small. Mature females are somewhat larger than even the biggest males. Forest duikers are different—both sexes have horns. Females are slightly bigger in body size. Duikers are usually solitary individuals.

Trophy Assessment — Estimating horn length: When a trophy-specimen bush duiker looks at you with its long and pointed ears cocked, horn tips that are level with the ear points are roughly four inches long. High-scoring

Duiker

trophies are those with horn tips that extend an inch or more above the level of the cocked ear points. Forest duiker horns vary greatly by species from just over 1 inch to over 7 inches for trophy specimens. SCI method (1A); RW method (7).

The Hunt — Duikers are difficult to hunt because of their super-refined senses, small size, neutral coloring, and their habit of staying in or close to long grass or thick bush. Duikers are commonly hunted with shotguns and are usually taken as short-range running targets as they break cover or when driven by beaters. Many are taken in chance encounters during hunts for something bigger. Still-hunting in known duiker habitat or ambushing a duiker at a likely feeding area at first light is also effective. Calling is the most productive method for forest duikers.

Rifle, Caliber, and Bullet Selection — Virtually all the hunting calibers—from the .22 centerfires with 45-grainers all the way up to the .375s and 300-grain softpoints—have been used with success on these diminutive antelope. A good scope is essential for the tricky light conditions under which many trophy duiker are taken. Shooting distances are usually short.

Shot Placement — A side-on high heart/lung shot is the most effective Place your shot on line of foreleg, just below body's midline. A quick-expanding bullet will make finding a downed trophy easier. A high shoulder/spinal shot will drop a duiker. Place shot high up and well forward on the shoulder, through the center of shoulder blade.

The Perfect Shot: Mini Edition for Africa II

Anatomy diagram.

Duiker

Klipspringer is the only species where the "liver shot" is recommended. Try not to hit the shoulder bones—the cape is easily ruined by such shots.

KLIPSPRINGER
Oreotragus oreotragus

Natural History — A klipspringer is known as the "ballerina of the rocks," and its name means "rock jumper." The klipspringer has the amazing agility to jump from rock to rock and effortlessly race up sheer cliff faces. Its body is covered with a dense layer of short, quill-like hairs. It is an important member of Africa's "small five" (with the bush duiker, grysbok, steenbok, and oribi). This highly sought-after trophy is exceedingly good eating and excellent bait for attracting leopard. Klipspringers occur in many of the continent's more arid and rugged mountain ranges. They are predominantly browsers. They are well suited to a dry, harsh environment, but drink when water is available. Most commonly encountered as individuals, in male/female pairs, or as small family groups. Most active during the cooler daylight hours. The alarm call of a klipspringer is a loud, shrill whistle.

Sex Determination — Normally only males carry horns. Females tend to be slightly bigger and a little heavier.

Trophy Assessment — Horns can be seen through a binocular even from a distance. Compare the length of the horn to that of the erect ears: Horns just above ear tips should be around 4 inches. SCI measurement (1A); RW method (7).

The Hunt — Look for suitably rocky terrain or mountain ranges. Hunt from bottom looking upward because klipspringers are used to predation from above. Their shrill alarm whistle often gives their presence away. Their habit of stopping to look back down at intruders provides a shooting opportunity. Climb slowly after them; they usually don't go far and prefer to keep their tormentor in sight. This can also provide a shooting opportunity.

Rifle, Caliber, and Bullet Selection — Requires only a .22 centerfire and a decently constructed 45- to 55-grain bullet, but they are usually hunted with heavier calibers up to the .375s. Overly fragile, high-velocity bullets can ruin a cape by blowing the quills out. In all calibers, solids are a good idea. A good scope and a quality binocular are essential for precise shot placement and trophy evaluation from a distance.

Shot Placement — Because klipspringers have vary fragile hollow hairs that damage easily, it is important to hit a klipspringer well behind the shoulder when shooting with a softpoint bullet—through the liver, in fact. This shot kills them quickly. Be careful not to hit the shoulder bones as the cape can easily be ruined by such shots; therefore, angled shots that could hit the shoulder bones should be avoided. Be patient and wait for side-on presentation before shooting.

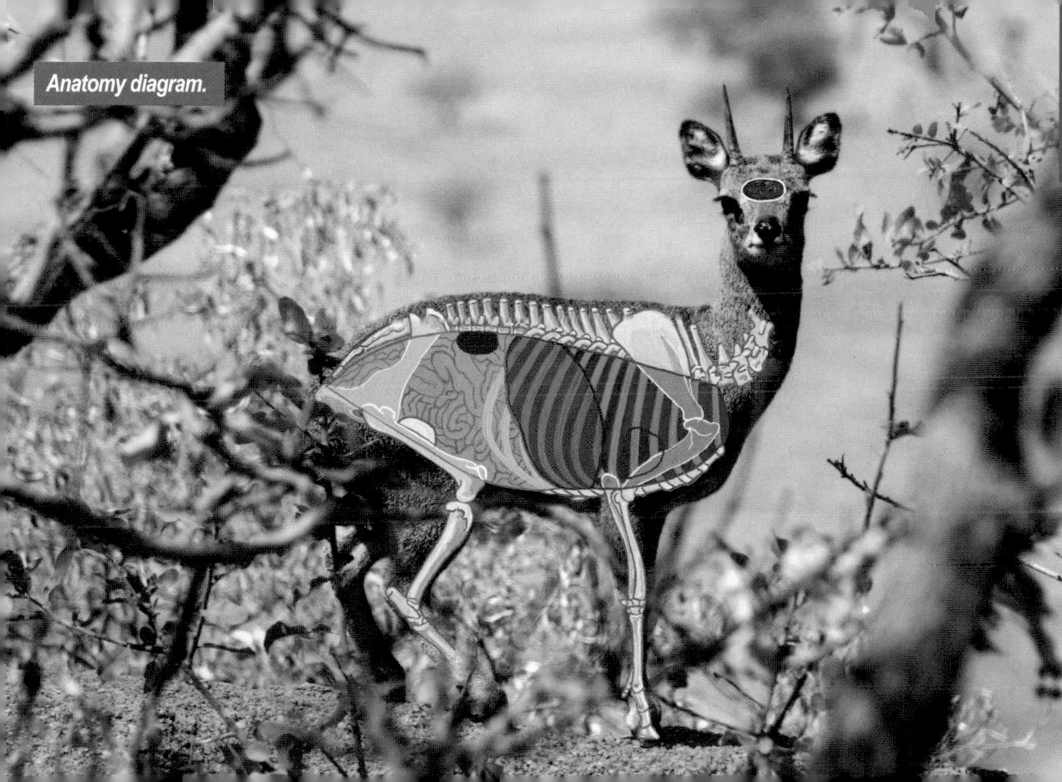

Anatomy diagram.

Steenbok

A high, behind-the-shoulder lung shot is the only shot-placement option.

STEENBOK
Raphicerus campestris

Natural History — The steenbok is a small, slim, and dainty, 25-pound antelope. It is common in the drier parts of Southern Africa and is an important member of the small five (along with duiker, klipspringer, oribi, and grysbok) and the tiny ten (oribi, suni, klipspringer, Damara dik-dik, Sharpe grysbok, Cape grysbok, red duiker, blue duiker, and common duiker). It is not water dependent, so it thrives in Southern Africa's most desolate areas. It is a mixed feeder and survives on grasses, seed pods, fruits, and forbs. It has a good sense of smell. It is active during daylight hours—early morning and late afternoon especially. It lies up during the heat of the day in thickets, under bushes, or in antbear burrows. Encountered as loners. Both sexes are strictly territorial.

Sex Determination — Only males carry horns, and these are smooth, widely spaced at the base, and grow vertically with sharp tips. Females have the same color and body shape and are often slightly larger.

Trophy Assessment — It is an easy species to evaluate. When a steenbok looks directly at you, the length of the head—from the horn bases to the lower jaw-line—is exactly 4 inches. When the horn tips are level with the ear, they are about 3 inches in length. Horns that are 4 inches are a good representative trophy, 4½ inches are really good, and 5 inches are exceptional. Horn bases are from 1½ to 2 inches. SCI method (1A): RW method (7).

Steenbok

The Hunt — A spot, walk, and stalk hunt is a real challenge because it's over open terrain with little cover, and steenboks are nervous and skittish. The steenbok is most active early morning and late in the afternoon; it is easier to approach when actively feeding or moving about. This antelope is territorial, so it's possible to find a good specimen again if initially unsuccessful. It will stop to look back after being spooked, so be ready.

Rifle, Caliber, and Bullet Selection — The steenbok is a dainty antelope and the skin can easily be damaged. It is usually shot at relatively close range, so the .22 Hornet and quality 45- to 55-grain bullets are ideal. Varmint-type bullets are too explosive and will ruin skin or cape. With the right bullets, a .222 Remington or a .223 is good choice. Use solids or super-premium expanding bullets in the larger calibers. Shooting distances are often overestimated. A good scope is necessary for correct shot placement.

Shot Placement — Only take the behind-the-shoulder, side-on lung shot and avoid hitting the shoulder bones. Since the steenbok is usually shot with overly large calibers, this shot is rapidly effective. Have patience to wait for side-on presentation. Angled shots are not recommended. Remember the skin is delicate and the cape is easily ruined.

Anatomy diagram.

Steenbok

A high lung shot is recommended for this delicate little antelope.

Grysbok

GRYSBOK

Raphicerus spp.

Natural History — There are two species, the Cape and the Sharpe grysbok. These tiny 15- to 18-pound antelopes have a grizzled appearance. They are solitary, shy, and secretive, and they prefer to hide rather than run away. They are rarely seen, so they are a real challenge to hunt. These two species are essential members of both the small five and tiny ten. While primarily browsers, they will also graze. They drink regularly. They do not occur in drier, more inhospitable areas. They are most active early morning and in late afternoon; they spend the heat of the day hiding in thick cover or in antbear holes.

Sex Determination — Only male grysboks carry short, widely spaced, thick-base horns. These are an inch or two in length. Body size and shape-wise, male and female grysbok look similar. The horns are the only way to determine sex.

Trophy Assessment — It's not easy to see horns that are only 1½ to 2 inches long. If you can see horns, they are usually a respectable trophy. Measured by SCI method (1A): RW method (7).

The Hunt — This secretive little antelope is rarely seen even in areas where the species is quite common. Most are taken from chance encounters while tracking or hunting something else. The most effective hunting method is to find a trophy-size specimen and then walk it up. Use a 12-gauge shotgun and a good "goose" load. Shoot as it bolts away.

Rifle, Caliber, and Bullet Selection — Grysboks are usually shot with whatever is being carried at the time of a chance encounter. A .22 Hornet and 45- to 55-grain solids are the perfect combination. The most popular option is a 12-gauge shotgun and a healthy duck or goose load.

Shot Placement —When rifles are used, the shoulder and front leg bones should be avoided. Do not make angled shots. Place the shot behind the shoulder into the top of the lungs. If you use a shotgun, don't shoot when too close.

The Perfect Shot: Mini Edition for Africa II

Side-on anatomy diagram.

Grysbok

Appendix I: Minimum requirements for inclusion in record book, number one record measurement and measurement system used, Safari Club International (SCI) and Roland Ward (RW).

(Both SCI and RW use inches and pounds; see end of chart for conversion information.)

Africa's Big Five	SCI			RW		
	Minimum	Record	Method	Minimum	Record	Method
Buffalo, Cape/southern	101	141	4	42	64	12
Buffalo, Central African savanna	65	96⅜	4	NC	NC	NC
Buffalo, dwarf forest	40	72½	4	20	29⅞	11
Buffalo, Nile	70	115⅜	4	38	44¼	12
Buffalo, West African savanna	55	94¼	4	37	46⅛	12
Elephant	90	302	14	80	226	16
Leopard	14	19¹¹⁄₁₆	15	15⅜	19	17
Lion	23	28¹⁄₁₆	15	24	28¾	17
Rhino, black	56	89¼	8	24	53½	15
Rhino, northern white	ED	67⅛	8	28	50⅛	15
Rhino, southern white	70	107⅜	8	28	62¼	15

ED=editor's discretion; NC=no category, NE-no entry.

	SCI			RW		
Other Game Animals	Minimum	Record	Method	Minimum	Record	Method
Blesbok	40	56⅜	1	16½	20⅝	7
Blesbok, white	39	52½	1	NC	NC	NC
Bontebok	37	47½	1	14	16¾	7
Bushbuck, Abyssinian	25	40¾	2	13⅜	NE	8
Bushbuck, Cape/South African	31	53½	2	15	20¼	8
Bushbuck, Chobe	33	55⅜	2	14	18¼	8
Bushbuck, East African	33	53	2	16	19¼	8
Bushbuck, harnessed	25	45	2	11¾	16⅛	8
Bushbuck, Limpopo	33	54⅜	2	15	20¼	8
Bushbuck, Masai	NC	NC	NC	16	19¼	8
Bushbuck, Menelik or Arusi	29	45¾	2	11⅜	15⅝	8
Bushbuck, Nile	29	45⁶⁄₈	2	13⅜	18¾	8
Bushbuck, Shoan	NC	NC	NC	11¼	14⅝	8
Bush Duiker, Angolan	11	15¾	1A	3	6½	7
Bush Duiker, East African	11	15¾	1A	3⅞	6⅛	7
Bush Duiker, southern	11	19¼	1A	4½	7⅛	7
Bush Duiker, western	10	15⅛	1A	3⅜	6¼	7
Crocodile, Nile	115"	18' 7"	16C	14	17	18
Duiker, Abbott	ED	15³⁄₁₆	1A	3	4⅜	7

ED=editor's discretion; NC=no category, NE-no entry.

Game Animals	SCI			RW		
	Minimum	Record	Method	Minimum	Record	Method
Duiker, Ader	NE	NE	NE	1	1½	7
Duiker, bay	5	17³⁄₁₆	1A	2⅜	4⅞	7
Duiker, black	ED	16⅜	1A	2⅜	6⅞	7
Duiker, black-fronted	ED	14⅛	1A	2½	4¾	7
Duiker, blue	4¼	9⅛	1A	1¾	2⅞	7
Duiker, Gabon/white-bellied	ED	16⅝	1A	2¾	5	7
Duiker, Harvey red	6	15⅛	1A	2½	5	7
Duiker, Jentink	ED	22½	1A	5	8⅜	7
Duiker, Maxwell	3	8¾	1A	1⅛	2⅝	7
Duiker, Natal red	8	13⅝	1A	2½	4⅛	7
Duiker, Ogilby	ED	16⅜	1A	3⅜	4⅞	7
Duiker, Peters	6	19¹⁄₁₆	1A	3	5⅞	7
Duiker, red-flanked	7	13⅝	1A	2½	4⅛	7
Duiker, Simpson	NC	NC	NC	1⅛	NE	7
Duiker, Weyns	ED	16⅝	1A	NC	NC	NC
Duiker, yellow-backed	13	22⅛	1A	4½	8⅜	7
Duiker, zebra	ED	12⅜	1A	1	2½	7
Eland, Central African giant	110	143⅜	2	44⅞	56¼	8
Eland, Cape	77	116¼	2	35	45	8

ED=editor's discretion; NC=no category, NE-no entry.

Game Animals	SCI			RW		
	Minimum	Record	Method	Minimum	Record	Method
Eland, East African	74	111⅜	2	33	42⅛	8
Eland, Livingstone	79	119	2	35	46⅝	8
Eland, West African giant	ED	NE	2	37¾	45½	8
Gemsbok, Angolan	82	94¼	1	35⅜	43⅝	7
Gemsbok, Kalahari	81	111⅝	1	40	49¼	7
Grysbok, Cape	5	13	1A	3	5¼	7
Grysbok, Sharpe	5	9¾	1A	1⅜	⅛	7
Hartebeest, Cape/red	62	81½	1	23	29½	7
Hartebeest, Coke	50	73	1	18⅞	24	7
Hartebeest, Hunter/hirola	ED	69⅜	1	23	28½	7
Hartebeest, Kenya highland	ED	66⅞	1	NC	NC	NC
Hartebeest, lelwel	60	76⅝	1	23	27⅝	7
Hartebeest, Lichtenstein	53	76	1	18½	24⅜	7
Hartebeest, Neumann	51	67¼	1	NC	NC	NC
Hartebeest, Swayne	ED	57½	1	16⅞	20¼	7
Hartebeest, tora	ED	NE	NE	19⅞	22⅞	7
Hartebeest, western	60	77¼	1	22½	28¾	7
Hippo, common	50	88³⁄₁₆	12	29⅞	64½	5
Hyena, spotted	15	20¹⁄₁₆	15	NC	NC	NC

ED=editor's discretion; NC=no category, NE-no entry.

Game Animals	SCI			RW		
	Minimum	Record	Method	Minimum	Record	Method
Impala, Angolan/black-faced	47	67⅞	1	20⅞	26¾	7
Impala, black	ED	55⅛	1	NC	NC	NC
Impala, East African	60	77¾	1	26⅜	36⅛	7
Impala, southern	52	69¾	1	23⅝	31⅞	7
Klipspringer	10	16⅞	1A	4⅛	6⅜	7
Kudu, Abyssinian greater	98	136⅜	2	42⅞	50⅛	8
Kudu, East African greater	109	145¾	2	52	59⅞	8
Kudu, Eastern Cape greater	98	141⅝	2	NC	NC	NC
Kudu, southern greater	121	155¾	2	53⅞	73⅞	8
Kudu, western greater	72	127⅛	2	42⅞	50⅛	8
Nyala, common	63	84⅝	2	27	32⅞	8
Nyala, mountain	75	117	2	30⅞	39½	8
Oryx, beisa	72	92⅞	1	30⅞	43	7
Oryx, fringe-eared	60	87⅝	1	30⅞	43⅜	7
Oryx, scimitar-horned	ED	105	1	38	50⅛	7
Reedbuck, Abyssinian Bohor	13	26¼	1B	8⅝	12¾	7
Reedbuck, common	21	35⅛	1B	14	19¼	7
Reedbuck, eastern Bohor	14	27½	1B	9½	14¾	7
Reedbuck, Nagor	ED	21⅜	1B	7½	11⅞	7

ED=editor's discretion; NC=no category, NE-no entry.

Game Animals	SCI			RW		
	Minimum	Record	Method	Minimum	Record	Method
Reedbuck, Nigerian Bohor	16	24⅞	1B	9	13	7
Reedbuck, Sudan Bohor	19	31⅜	1B	13	16¾	7
Mountain reedbuck, Chanler	8	15½	1B	6⅛	9⅝	7
Mountain reedbuck, southern	11	18¼	1B	6⅞	10	7
Roan, Angolan	NC	NC	NC	27	34	7
Roan, East African	58	83¾	1	27	32¾	7
Roan, southern	67	86⅜	1	27	39	7
Roan, Sudan	68	82⅜	1	27	37¼	7
Roan, western	63	89⅝	10	27	36¼	7
Sable, common or typical	96	128⅜	1	41⅞	55⅜	7
Sable, giant/royal	ED	141⅞	1	55⅞	64⅞	7
Sable, Roosevelt	61	114⅝	1	33⅞	44¾	7
Springbok, Angolan	34	39⅞	1	NC	NC	NC
Springbok, black	30½	47⅞	1	NC	NC	NC
Springbok, Copper	ED	43⅝	1	NC	NC	NC
Springbok, Kalahari	35	52½	1	14	19⅜	7
Springbok, South African	30	47½	1	NC	NC	NC
Springbok, white	28	43⅝	1	NC	NC	NC
Steenbok	8	17⅞	1A	4½	7½	7

ED=editor's discretion; NC=no category, NE-no entry.

Game Animals	SCI			RW		
	Minimum	Record	Method	Minimum	Record	Method
Warthog	29	49⅝	12	13	24	6
Waterbuck, Angolan defassa	63	75⅝	1	24	36⅛	7
Waterbuck, common/ringed	67	92⅜	1	28	39¼	7
Waterbuck, Crawshay defassa	55	77⅜	1	25	31¼	7
Waterbuck, East African defassa	64	87⅞	1	27	35	7
Waterbuck, sing-sing	ED	85	1	27	36¼	7
Waterbuck, Ugandan defassa	NC	NC	NC	33⅞	39¼	7
Wildebeest, black/white-tailed	72	101¼	6	22⅞	29⅜	13
Wildebeest, blue/brindled	70	99¼	5	28½	33⅞	12
Wildebeest, Cookson	70	94⅝	5	NC	NC	NC
Wildebeest, Nyasa	ED	95⅛	5	28	33⅛	12
Wildebeest, white-bearded	68	94⅛	5	28	32	12

ED=editor's discretion; NC=no category, NE-no entry.

Records are according to *SCI Record Book of Trophy Animals*, Ed. XII, Vol. 1 & 2, 2011; *Rowland Ward's Records of Big Game*, 29th edition, 2014.

Conversions: 1 inch = 2.54 centimeters; 1 pound = 454 grams.

See Appendix II and III for explanation of measurement methods.

Appendix II: Measurement Methods Used by Safari Club International

SCI started its measurement system in 1977 in Tucson, Arizona. In the beginning it was largely a book for club members only, but it has now grown well beyond this. Its measurement methods for African game are relatively simple. A book with listings of animal measurements and the hunters who have shot them is issued every few years. SCI currently (2015) has thirteen editions in print. We list only the SCI methods that are applicable to African animals in this book. (This is only a synopsis of the SCI system; for a full description, we refer you to the SCI Record Book of Trophy Animals.)

Method 1 (for animals with simple horns) — Length of horns (left and right) plus circumferences of horns at bases (left and right), to nearest ⅛ inch.

Method 1A (for small animals with simple horns) — Length of horns (left and right) plus circumferences of horns at bases (left and right), to nearest 1/16 inch.

Method 2 (for animals with spiraled horns) — Length of horns (left and right) along spiral ridge plus circumferences of horns at bases (left and right), to nearest ⅛ inch.

Method 4 (for African buffalo) — From left tip to right tip of horns along bottom of horns plus width of each boss to nearest ⅛ inch.

Method 5 (for common wildebeest) — From left tip to right tip of horns along bottom of horns across forehead plus circumference of boss of each horn to nearest ⅛ inch.

Method 6 (for black wildebeest) — Start at horn tip, measure to the bottom of the first curve, come up behind to the top of the boss, cross the gap of the horns to the other boss and continue in a same manner to the other horn tip. Add to this the widths of both bosses.

Method 8 (for rhino) — Length of front horn plus circumference of front horn at base. Add to this length of rear horn plus circumference of rear horn at base, to nearest 1/8 inch.

Method 12 (for hippo and warthog) — Length of both lower tusks on outer curve plus circumference of both tusks at largest place, to nearest 1/16 inch.

Method 14 (for elephant) — Weight of left and right tusks to nearest ½ pound.

Method 15 (for carnivores) — Length of skull plus width of skull to nearest 1/16 inch.

Method 16C (for crocodiles) — Length of body, including tail, up over the top line of the body, to nearest ½ inch.

Appendix III: Measurement Methods Used by Rowland Ward

Rowland Ward, owner of the most famous taxidermy studio of his time, started this measurement system in 1892 in London. The measurement methods are very simple, and many require the length of only one antler or horn. A book with listings of animal measurements and the hunters who have shot them is issued every three to four years. RW currently (2014) has twenty-nine editions in print. We list only the RW methods that are applicable to African animals in this book. Please note that RW requires a number of supplemental measurements that are not used in the ranking and, for reasons of brevity, are not listed here. (This is only a synopsis of the RW system; for a full description we refer you to Rowland Ward's Records of Big Game.)

Method 5 (for hippo) — Length of the longest lower tusk.

Method 6 (for warthog) — Length of the longest upper tusk.

Method 7 (for species with simple, unbranched horns) — Length of the longest horn along front curve.

Method 8 (for spiral-horned species) — Length of the longest horn along the spiral ridge.

Method 11 (for dwarf buffalo) — Length of the longest horn on outside curve.

Method 12 (for all other buffalo and common wildebeest) — Width of outside spread along straight line at right angles to the axis of the skull.

Method 13 (for black wildebeest) — Length of the longest horn. Measure by starting at the bottom of the boss, go with the grain of the horn to the tip.

Method 15 (for rhino) — Length of the longest horn measured along the front curve.

Method 16 (for elephant) — Weight of the single heaviest tusk.

Method 17 (for carnivores) — Length of skull added to width of skull.

Method 18 (for crocodiles) — Field measurement, before skinning. Pull the nose and tail to get them into a straight line. (Make sure crocodile is dead!) Then drive in pegs at the end of the nose and tail. Take the measurements between pegs and NOT following the line of the body, to nearest ¼ inch.

Appendix IV: Selected Tracks

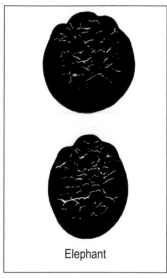

Elephant

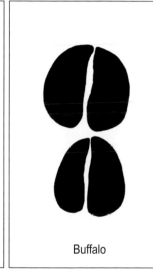

Buffalo

Hippopotamus

(Top: front foot; bottom: rear foot. Not to scale)

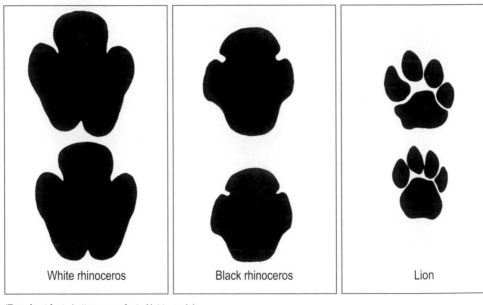

| White rhinoceros | Black rhinoceros | Lion |

(Top: front foot; bottom: rear foot. Not to scale)

The Perfect Shot: Mini Edition for Africa II

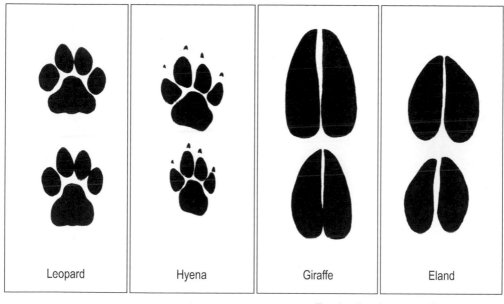

Leopard | Hyena | Giraffe | Eland

(Top: front foot; bottom: rear foot. Not to scale)

The Perfect Shot: Mini Edition for Africa II

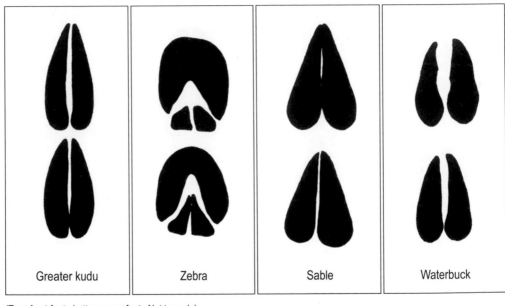

| Greater kudu | Zebra | Sable | Waterbuck |

(Top: front foot; bottom: rear foot. Not to scale)

The Perfect Shot: Mini Edition for Africa II

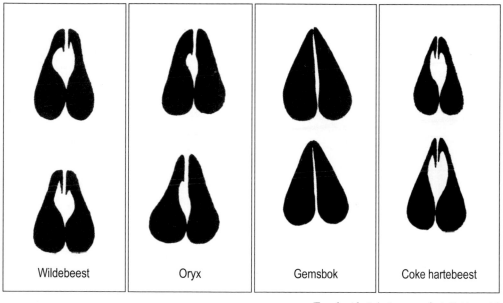

| Wildebeest | Oryx | Gemsbok | Coke hartebeest |

(Top: front foot; bottom: rear foot. Not to scale)

The Perfect Shot: Mini Edition for Africa II

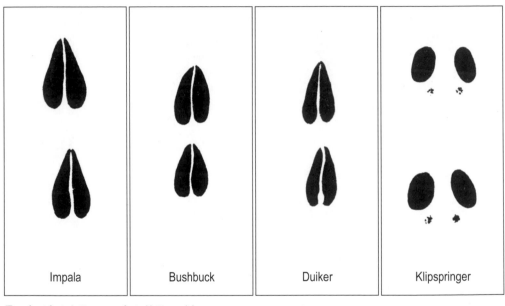

| Impala | Bushbuck | Duiker | Klipspringer |

(Top: front foot; bottom: rear foot. Not to scale)

The Perfect Shot: Mini Edition for Africa II

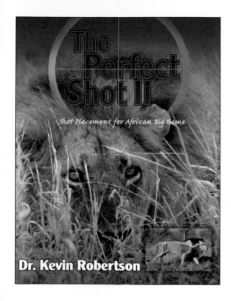

Dr. Kevin Robertson

www.safaripress.com

The Perfect Shot: Mini Edition for Africa II